Phonics Wonder

LEVEL 2

Short Vowels

Contents

Lesson Plans of Phonics Wonder

Lesson Plan

Letter & Sound
New target combinations of sounds and related words are introduced with pictures.

Read
Children practice reading words with the target sounds.

Listen & Write
Children practice identifying and writing the target sounds.

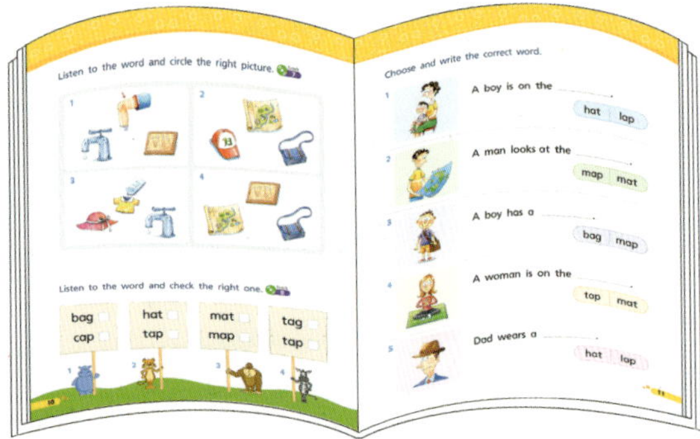

Listen & Read
Children practice listening and reading the target words.

Read
Children practice reading sentences with the target words.

Read Along!
Children further practice the target words reading simple story.

Write Words
Children confirm their understanding of the target sounds and words by writing them.

Key Features

Review 1 — The Review provides practice of the materials from the previous two units by using a variety of exercises for the target sounds of letters and words.

Final Review — The Final Review reinforces the material with a variety of exercises such as the reading of brief stories that include the sight words and playing games.

Final Test — The Final Test consists of 20 listening comprehension questions and 16 reading questions that cover the target sounds of letters and words.

Introduction of the Multi-ROM

 **Sound**
Children practice the target sounds and the corresponding words.

 **Words**
Children listen and repeat the words with the target sounds.

 **Chant**
Children listen and repeat the target sounds and words in the chant.

Read Along
 Children read and repeat the key words with the target letters in the sentences.

Game
 Children play games using the target letters and words.

Check-Up
 Children take a brief test by listening and reading the target letters and words.

Details

 Children listen and repeat the target sounds and words by watching the shape of a native speaker's mouth.

 In **Words** corner, children write the target words by clicking their mouses.

 Children record their own pronunciation of the target words and check it by comparing it to the recording of a native speaker's pronunciation.

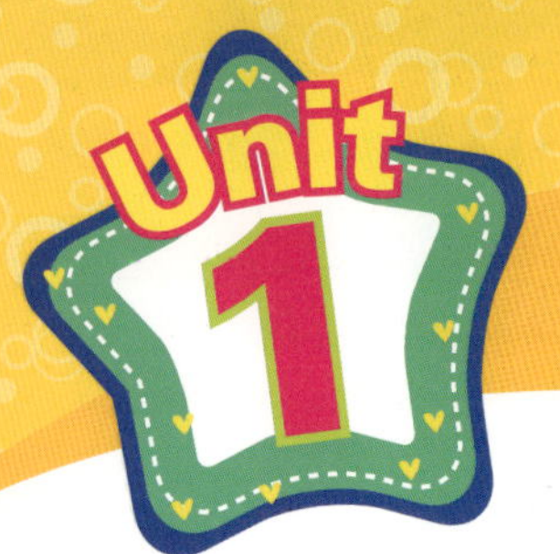

Unit 1 short vowel a

Listen and repeat. Track 1

a p → a p → c a p

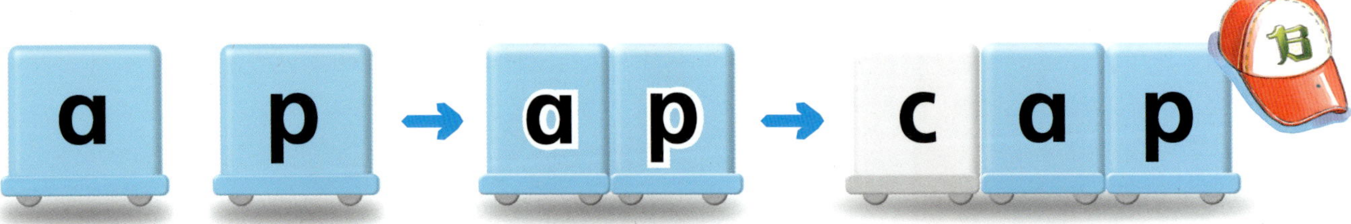

Track 2

-ap

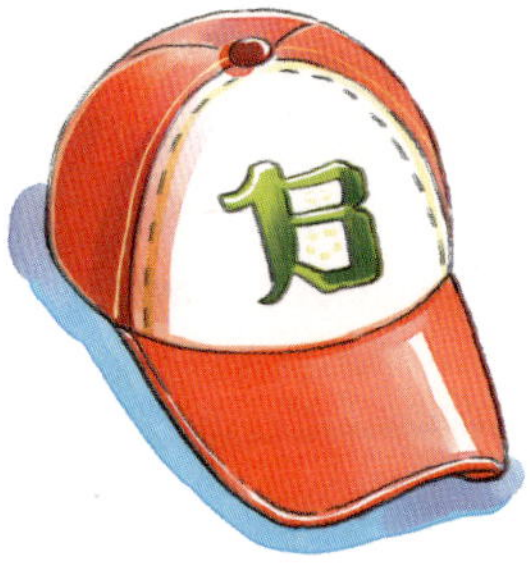

c ap **cap**

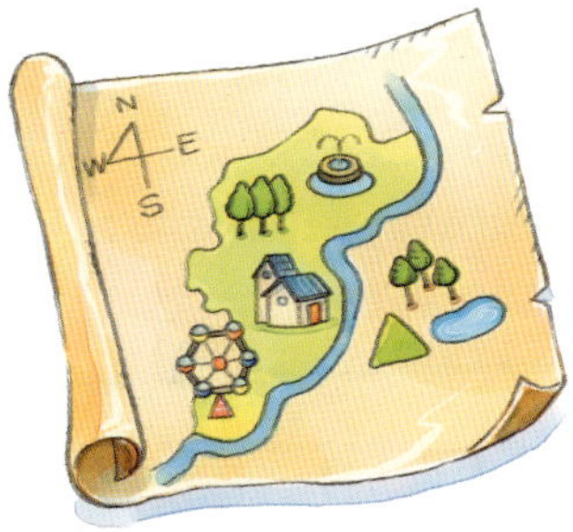

m ap **map**

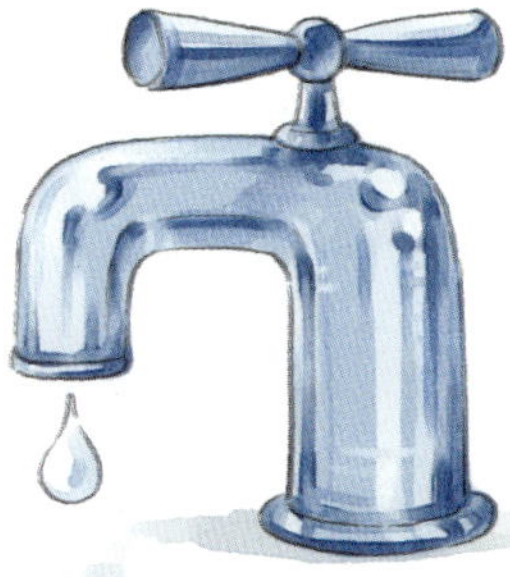

t ap **tap**

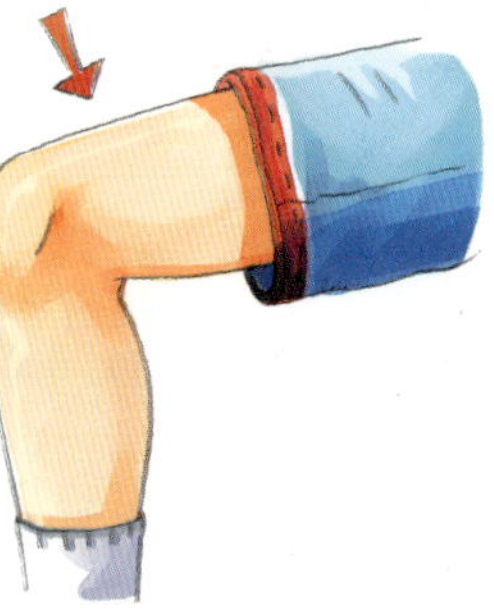

l ap **lap**

Listen and repeat. **Track 3**

a · t → a t → h a t

a · g → a g → b a g

Track 4

-at

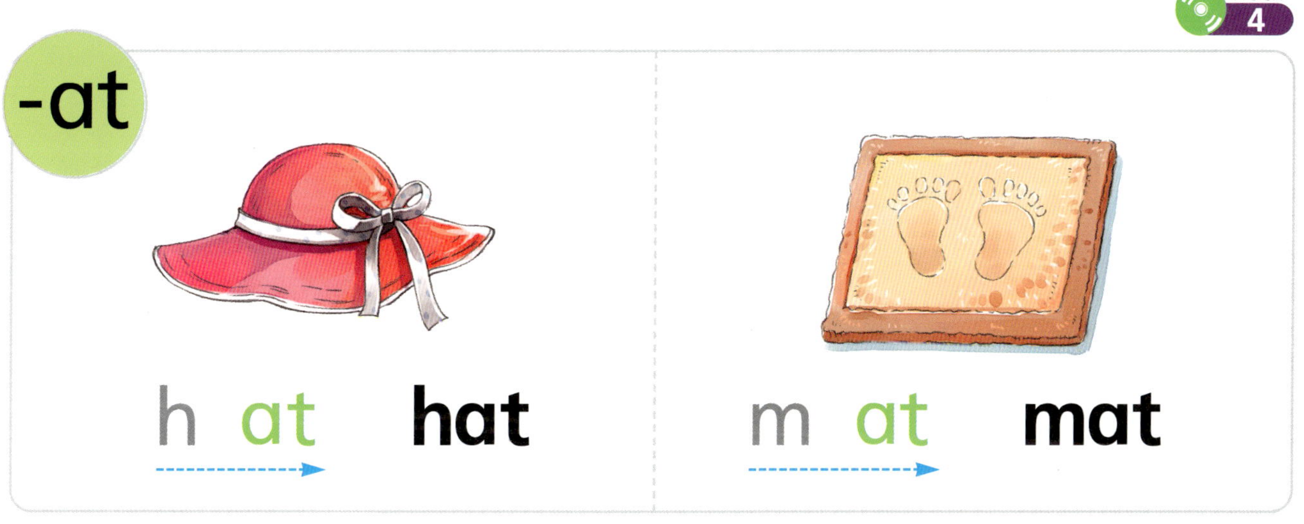

h at **hat**

m at **mat**

-ag

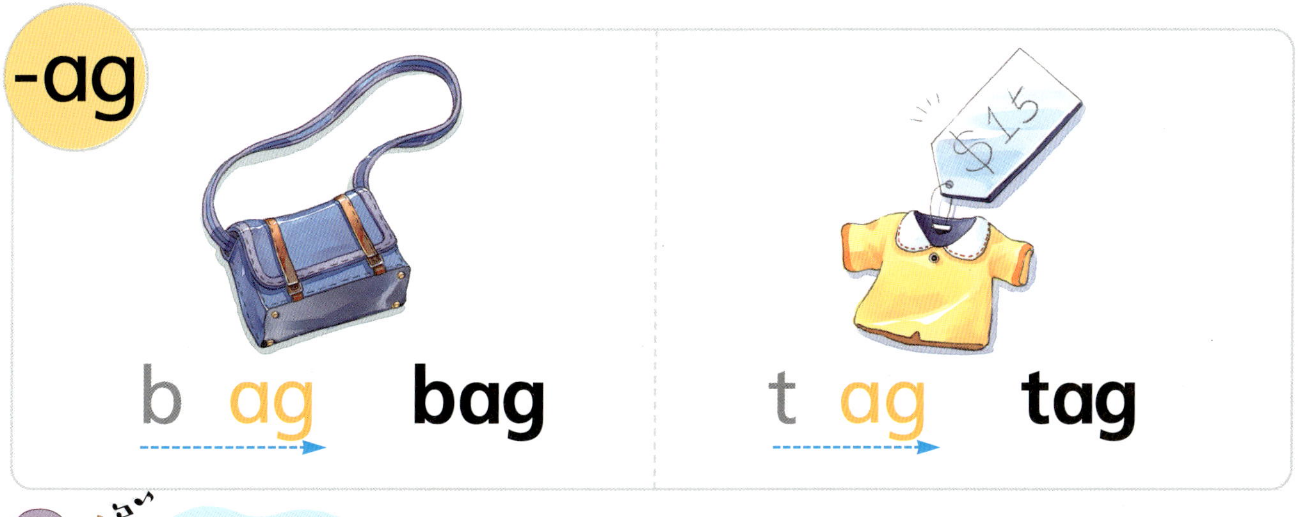

b ag **bag**

t ag **tag**

Let's chant! **Track 5**

Read the word and circle the right picture.

1 lap

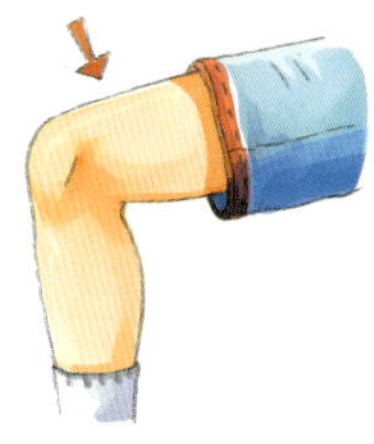  

2 hat

3 tap

4 bag

 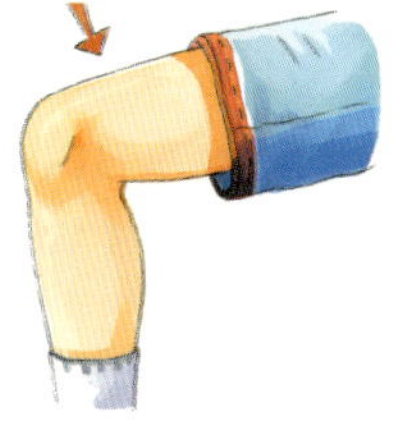 

5 mat

6 tag

Listen to the word and choose the rhyme. Then write it. 

1

at   ag   ap

h

2

at   ag   ap

l

3

at   ag   ap

t

4

at   ag   ap

t

5

at   ag   ap

m

6

at   ag   ap

b

Listen to the word and circle the right picture. 

Listen to the word and check the right one.

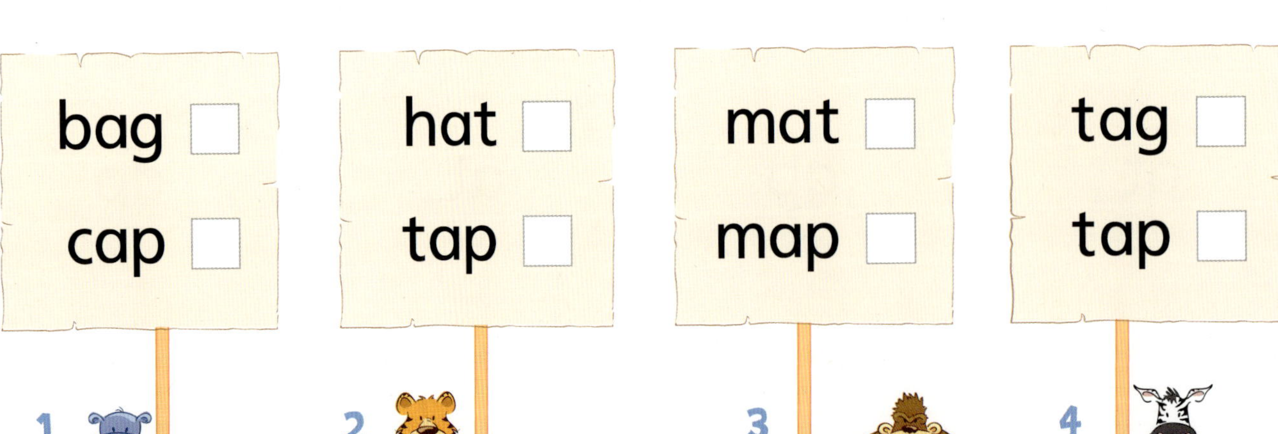

Choose and write the correct word.

1

A boy is on the ____________.

| hat | lap |

2

A man looks at the ____________.

| map | mat |

3

A boy has a ____________.

| bag | map |

4

A woman is on the ____________.

| tap | mat |

5

Dad wears a ____________.

| hat | lap |

Where is the map?

The map is on my lap.

Where is the tag?

The tag is on my bag.

Where is the hat?

The hat is on the mat.

Write the words.

-ap

cap

map

tap

lap

-at

hat

mat

-ag

bag

tag

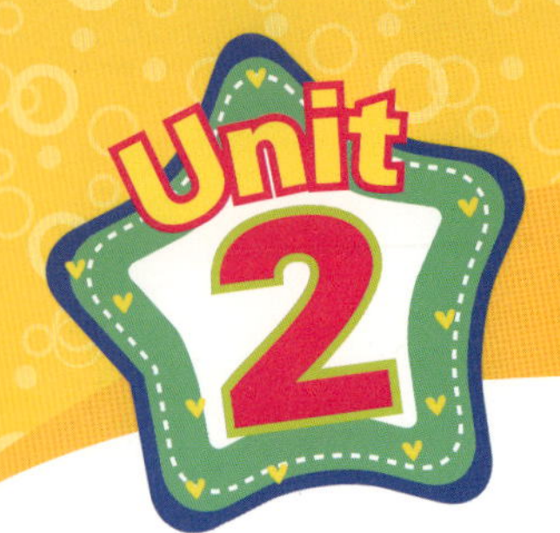

Unit 2 short vowel a

Listen and repeat. Track 10

a n → an → man

Track 11

-an

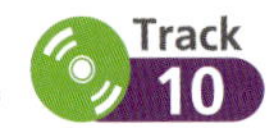

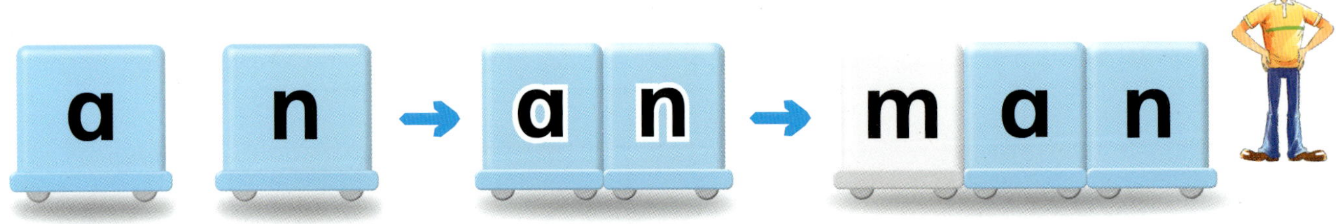

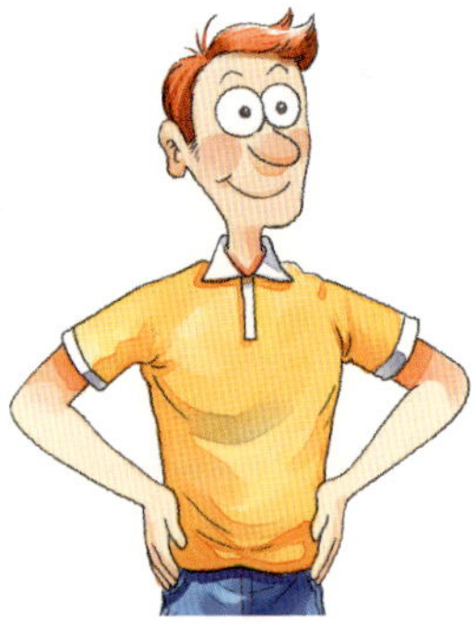

m an → man

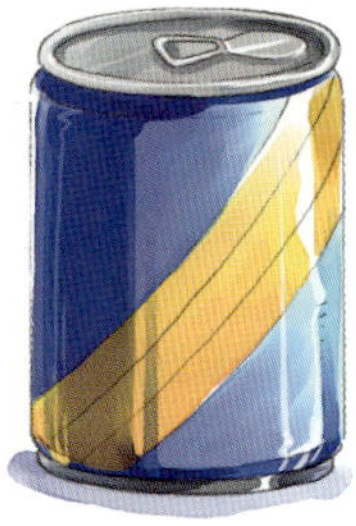

c an → can

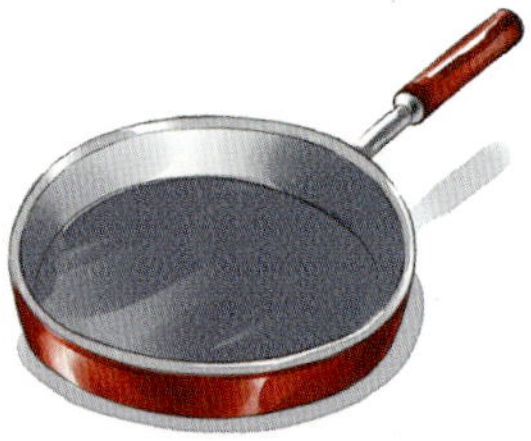

p an → pan

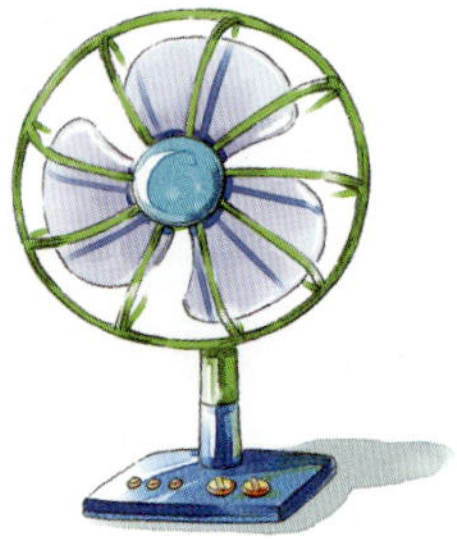

f an → fan

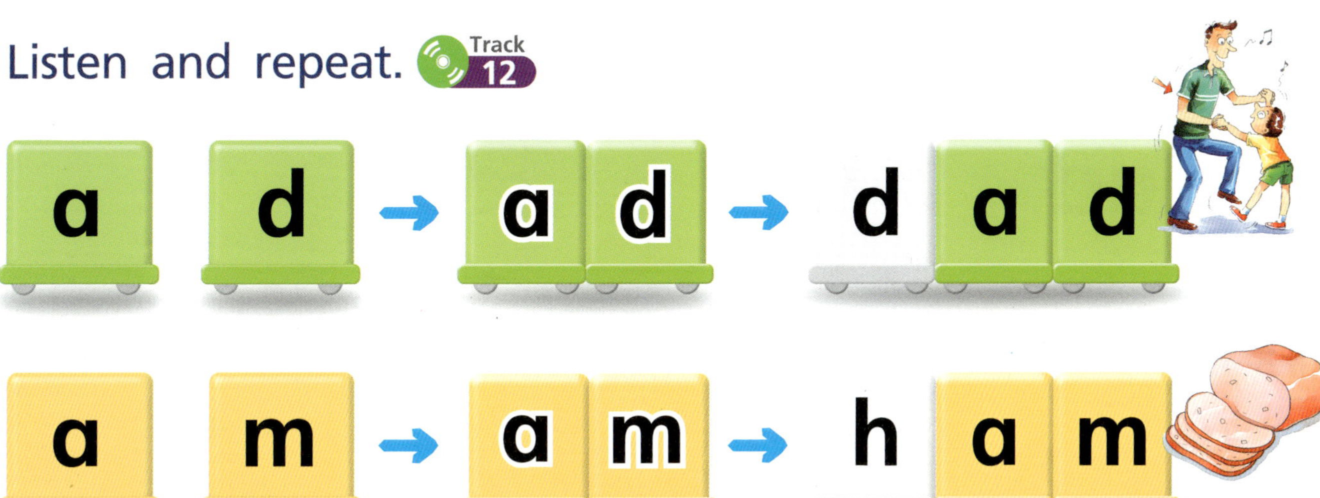

a d → a d → d a d

a m → a m → h a m

Track 13

-ad

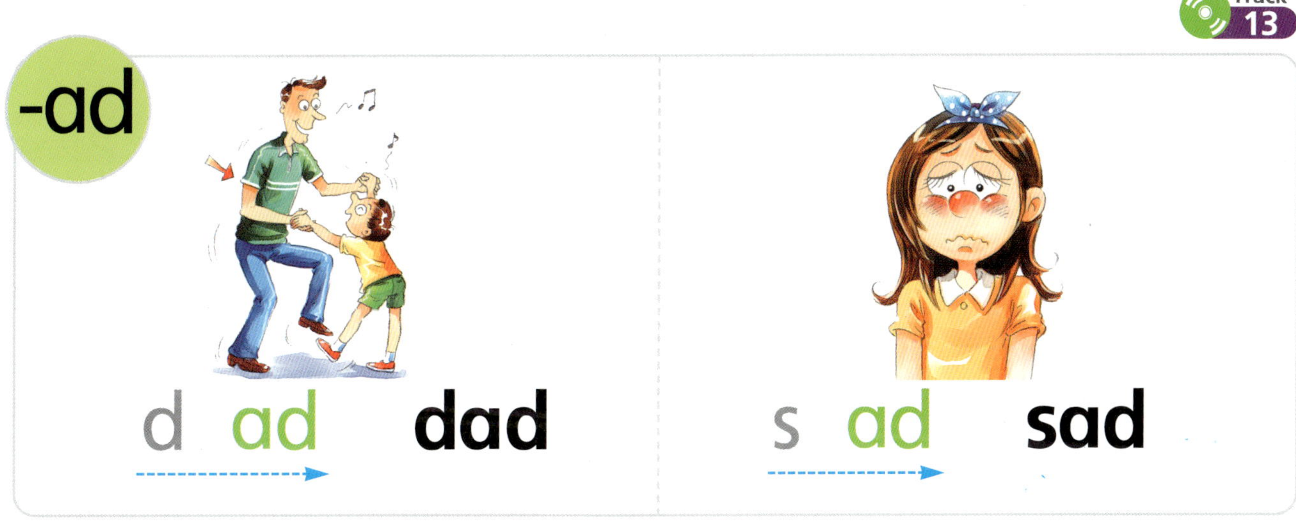

d ad **dad**

s ad **sad**

-am

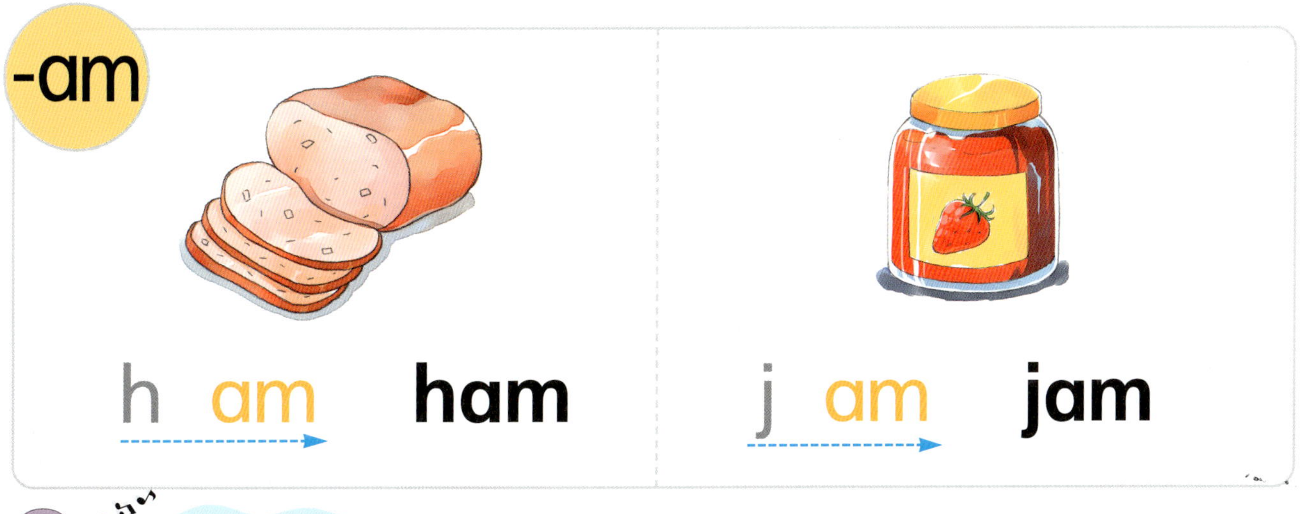

h am **ham**

j am **jam**

Let's chant! Track 14

Read the word and circle the right picture.

1 sad   

2 pan   

3 fan   

4 jam   

5 man   

6 dad   

Listen to the word and choose the rhyme. Then write it. 

1

an   ad   am

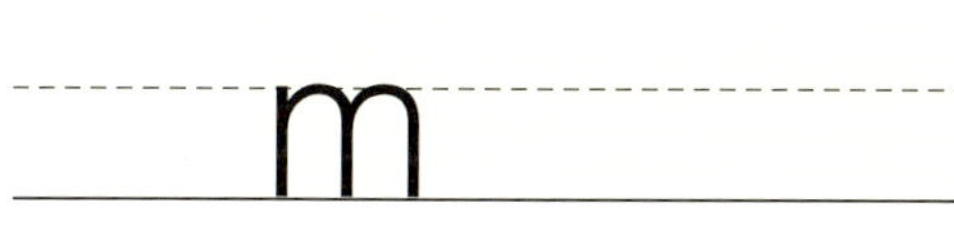

2

an   ad   am

h

3

an   ad   am

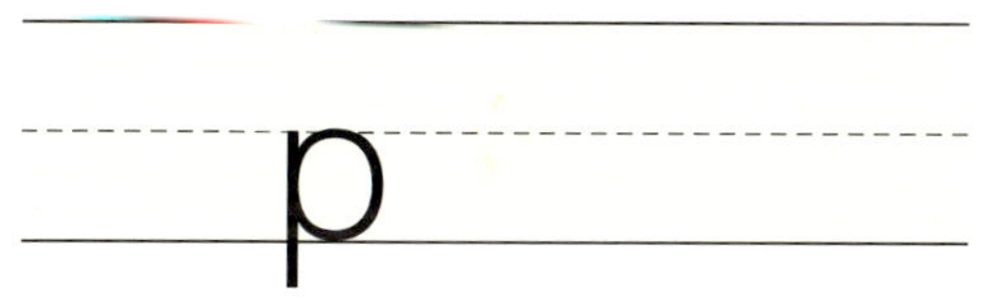

4

an   ad   am

d

5

an   ad   am

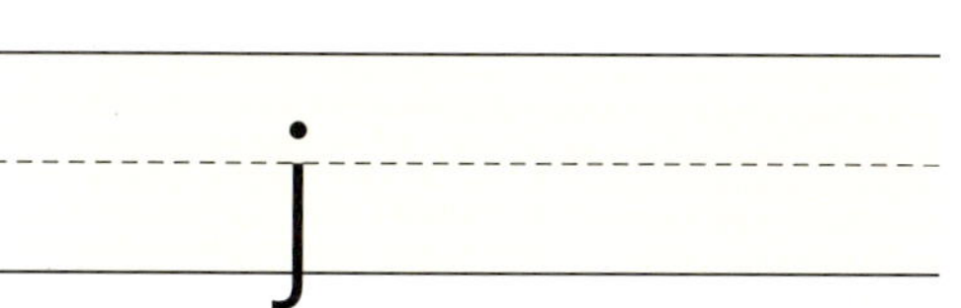

6

an   ad   am

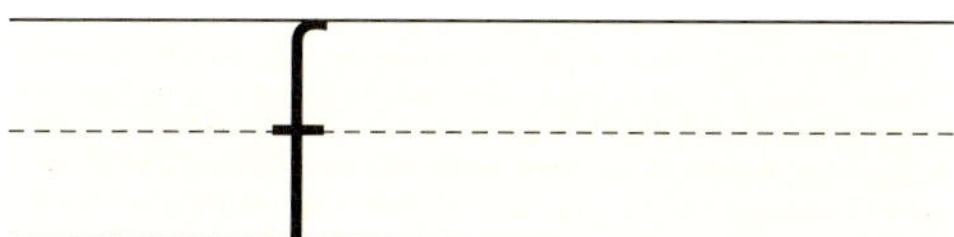

Listen to the word and circle the right picture. 

Listen to the word and check the right one.

Choose and write the correct word.

1

Jenny is ____________ and she cries.

| sad | fan |

2

Bread and ____________ is delicious.

| jam | can |

3

A ____________ is on the mat.

| man | ham |

4

The ham is in the ____________.

| dad | pan |

5

John opens the ____________.

| can | fan |

Track
18

Sam has ham.

Sam has jam.

Who has ham and jam?

Sam has ham and jam.

Ann has a can.

Ann has a pan.

Who has a can and a pan?

Ann has a can and a pan.

Write the words.

-an

man

can

pan

fan

-ad

dad

sad

-am

ham

jam

Match each rhyme with right pictures.

1 -ap ·  · 

2 -ad ·  · 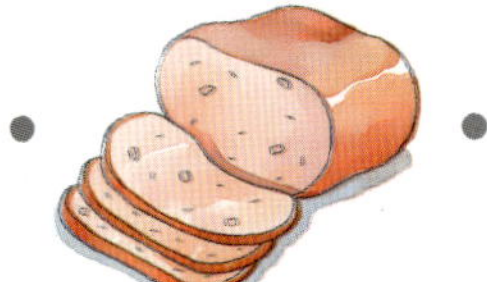

3 -at ·  · 

4 -an ·  · 

5 -ag ·  · 

6 -am ·  ·

Listen to the word and circle the right picture. Track 19

1 

2  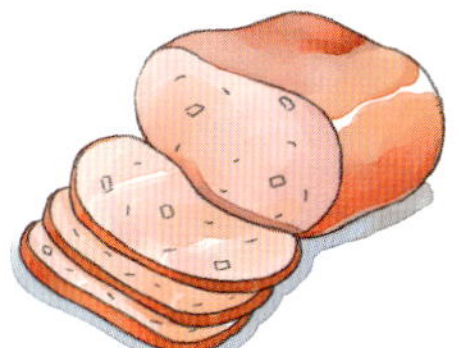

3 

4  

5  

6  

Listen to the word and circle the right one. Track 20

1   tag   can   cap

2   bag   pan   tag

3   hat   dad   can

4   fan   mat   tag

5   jam   man   mat

6   map   man   ham

Listen to the word and match the letter to the right rhyme. Then write the word. Track 21

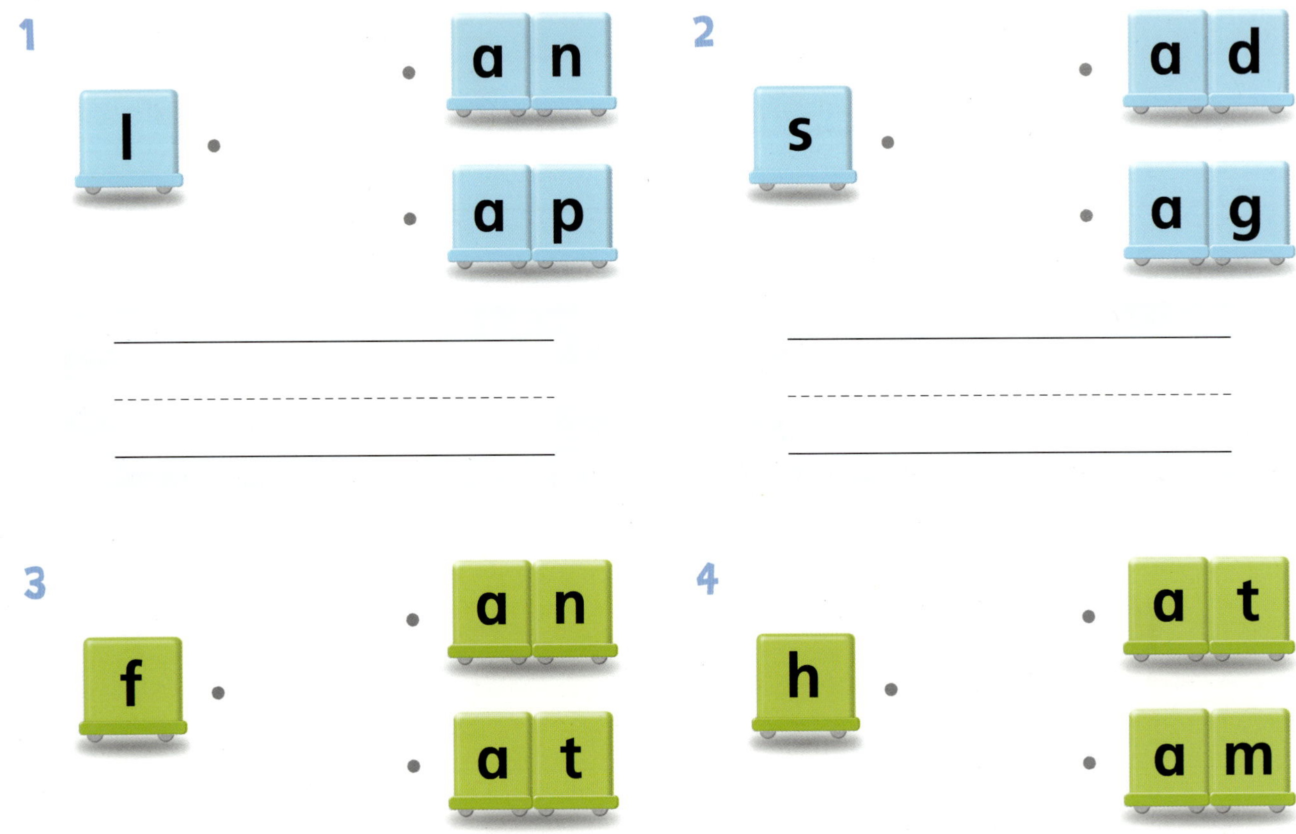

1

l

• a n

• a p

____

2

s

• a d

• a g

____

3

f

• a n

• a t

____

4

h

• a t

• a m

____

5

c

• a n

• a p

____

6

m

• a p

• a n

____

Look at the picture and write the word in the puzzle.

Unit 3 — short vowel **i**

Listen and repeat. **Track 22**

Track 23

-ig

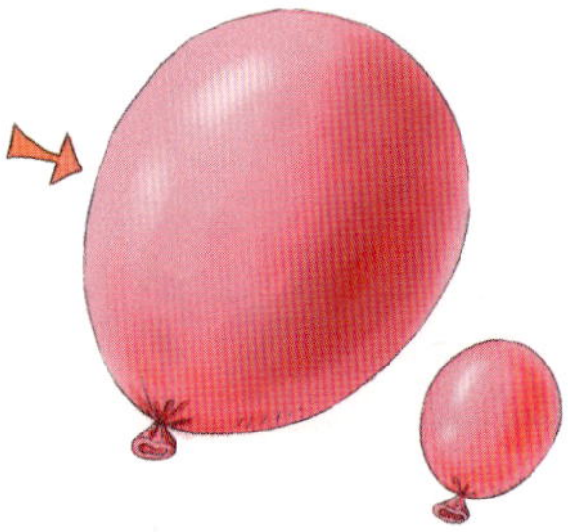

b ig **big**

p ig **pig**

d ig **dig**

w ig **wig**

Listen and repeat. Track 24

i p → i p → h i p

Track 25

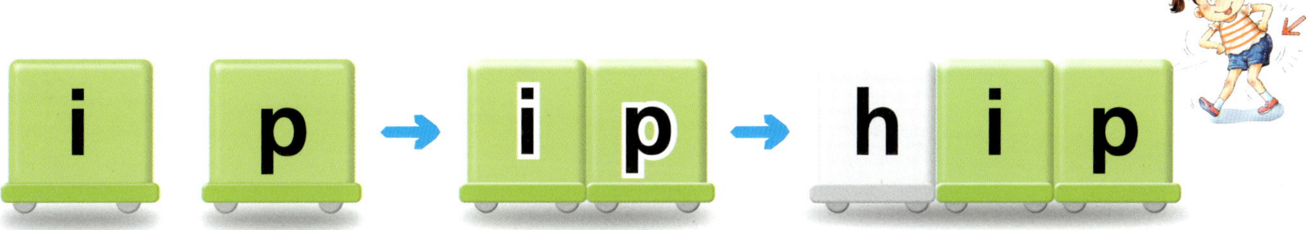

-ip

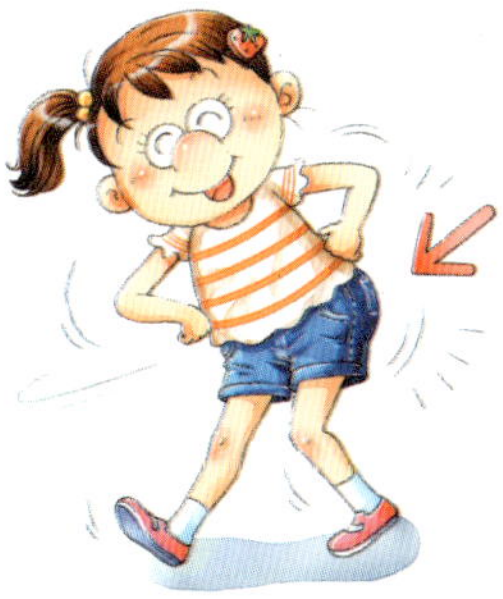

h ip hip

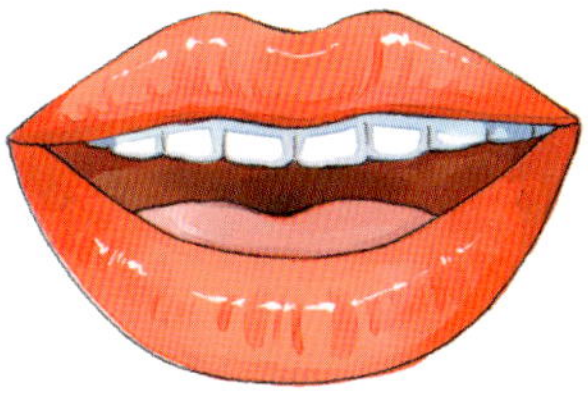

l ip lip

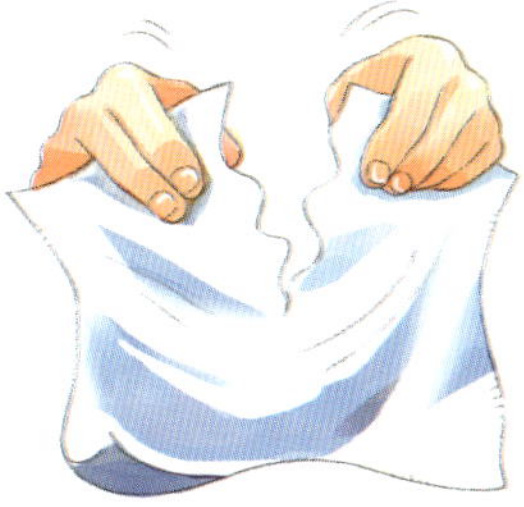

r ip rip

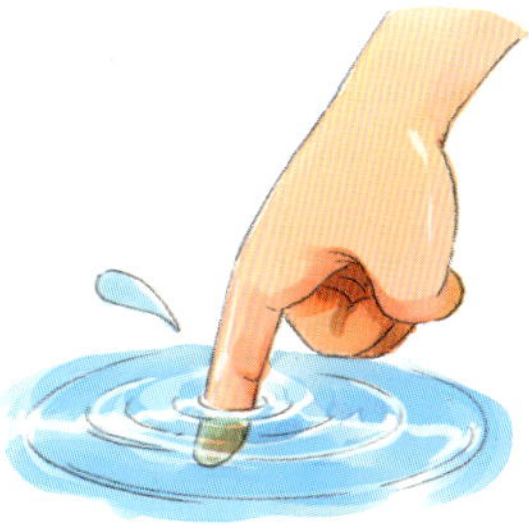

d ip dip

Let's chant! Track 26

Read the word and circle the right picture.

1 big

2 hip

3 pig

 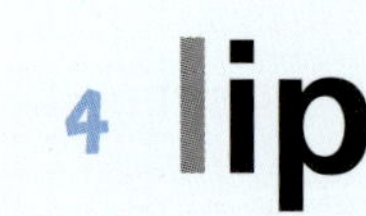

4 lip

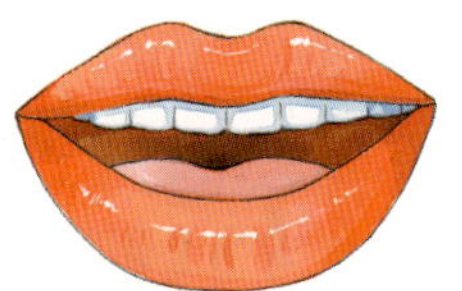 

5 dig

6 dip

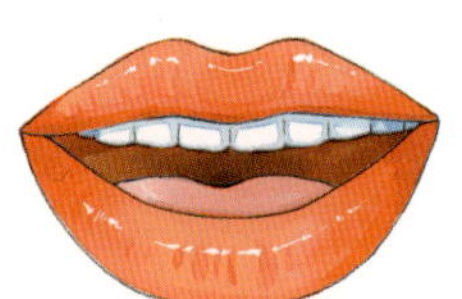

Listen to the word and choose the rhyme. Then write it. 

1

ig   ip

b

2

ig   ip

r

3

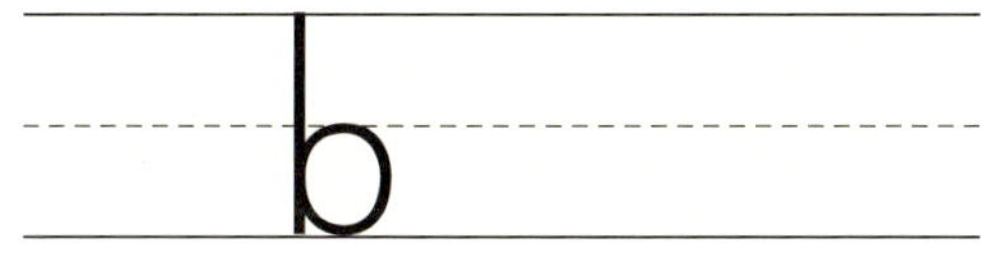

ig   ip

p

4

ig   ip

d

5

ig   ip

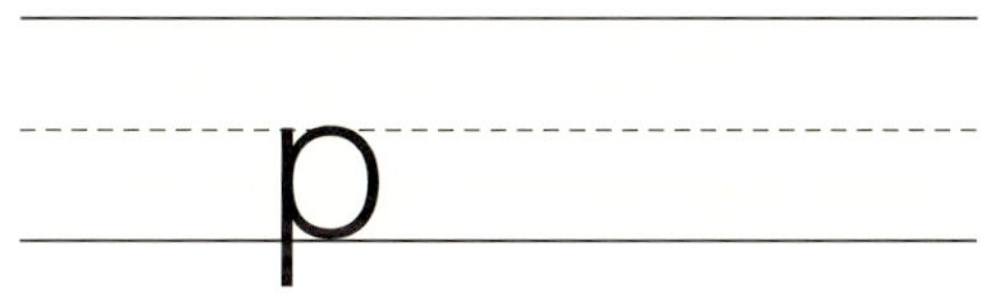

w

6

ig   ip

l

Listen to the word and circle the right picture. Track 28

1

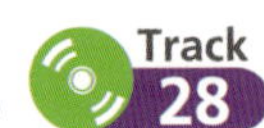

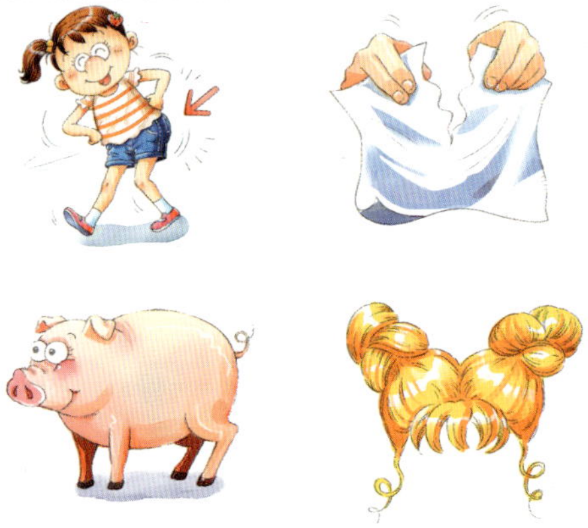

2

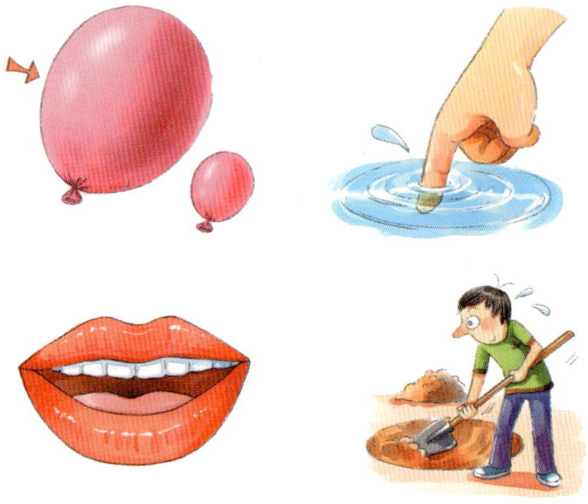

3

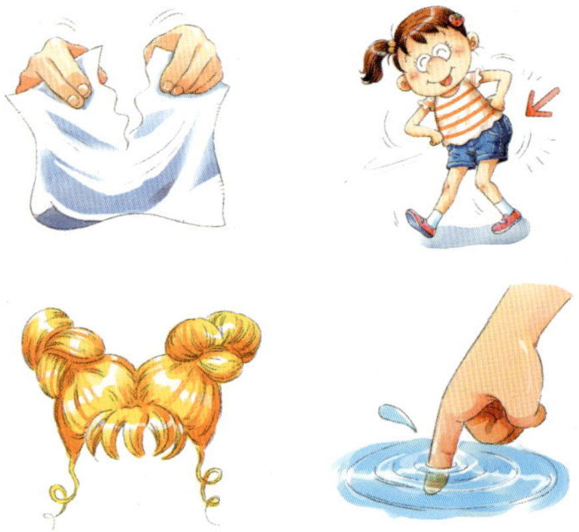

4

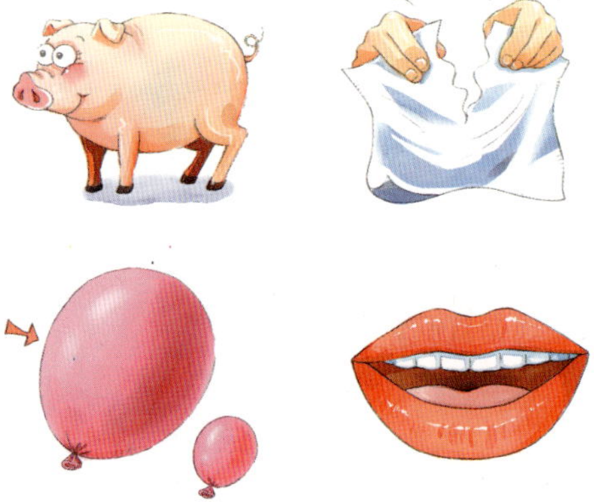

Listen to the word and check the right one. Track 29

1	2	3	4
pig ☐	wig ☐	dig ☐	dig ☐
hip ☐	rip ☐	dip ☐	lip ☐

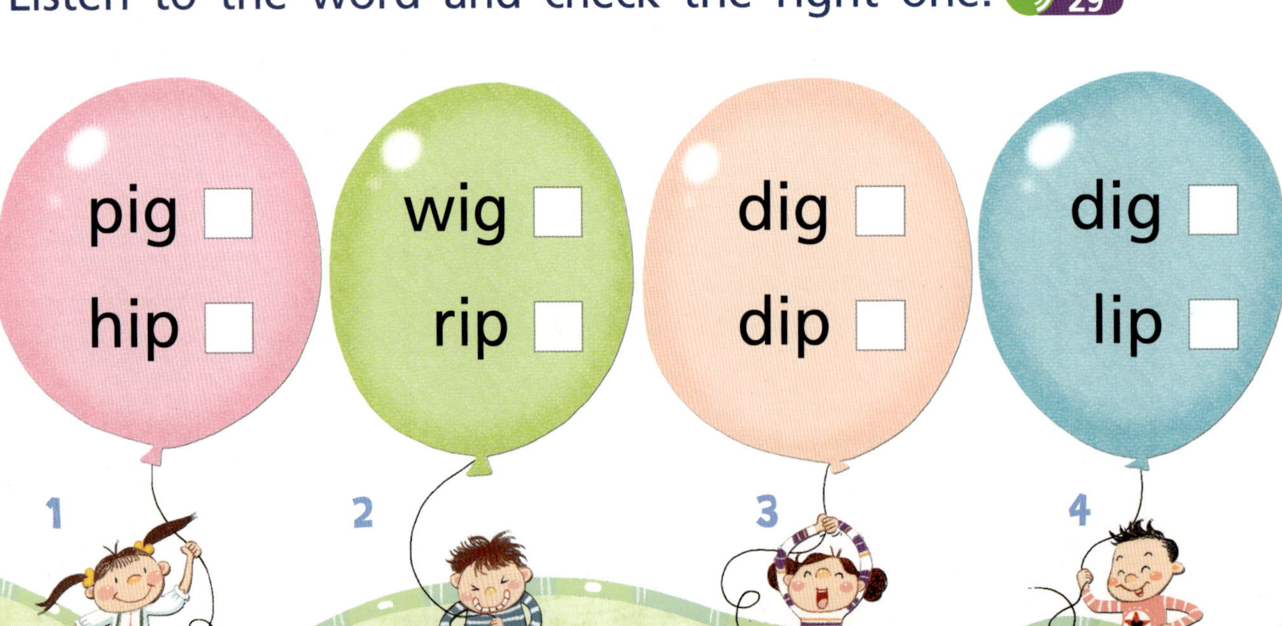

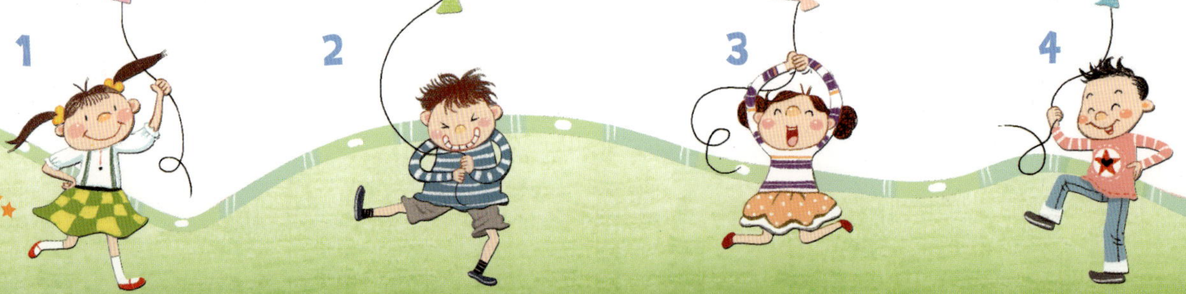

Choose and write the correct word.

1 

A girl wears a ___________ .

| wig | hip |

2 

A man __________s the paper.

| dig | rip |

3 

A ___________ is inside a fence.

| pig | lip |

4 

Kelly __________s her finger into the water.

| big | dip |

5

Mary wears ___________ sunglasses.

| lip | big |

The pig is in a wig.

Now he begins to dig.

Look what he makes!

A hole that is large.

The pig has big hips.

Now he begins to rip.

Look what he makes!

A mess that is big.

Write the words.

-ig

big

pig

dig

wig

-ip

hip

tip

rip

dip

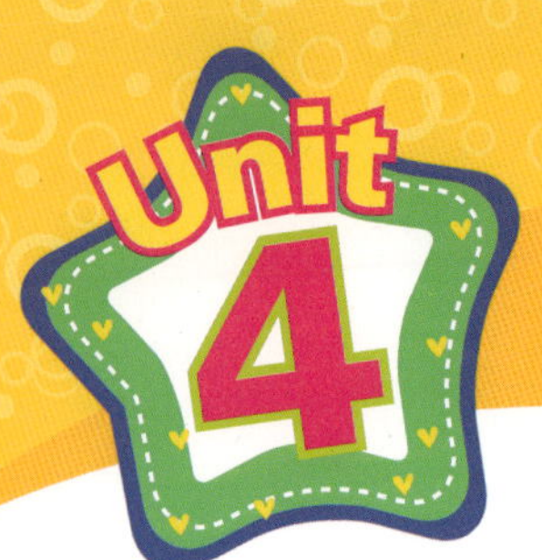

Unit 4

short vowel i

Listen and repeat. Track 31

i n → in → bin

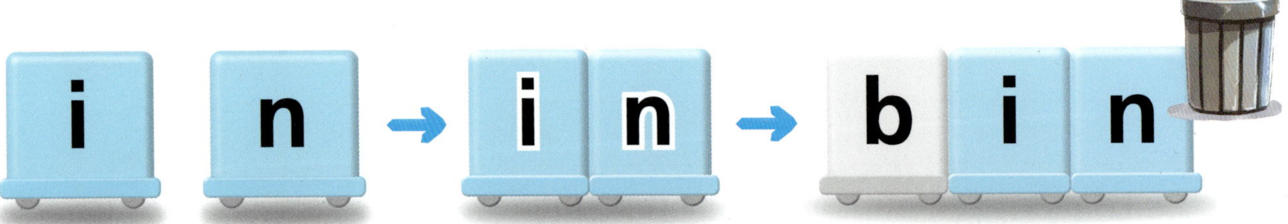

Track 32

-in

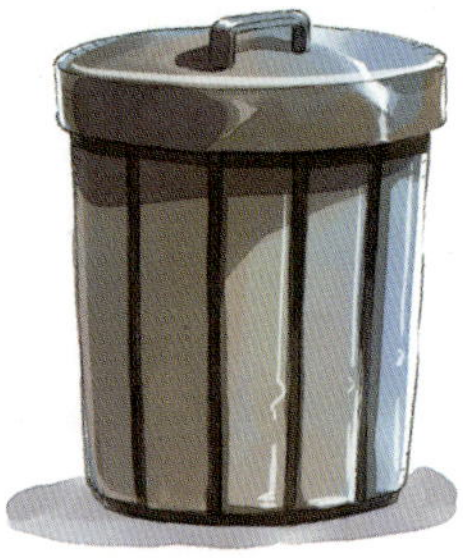

b in **bin**

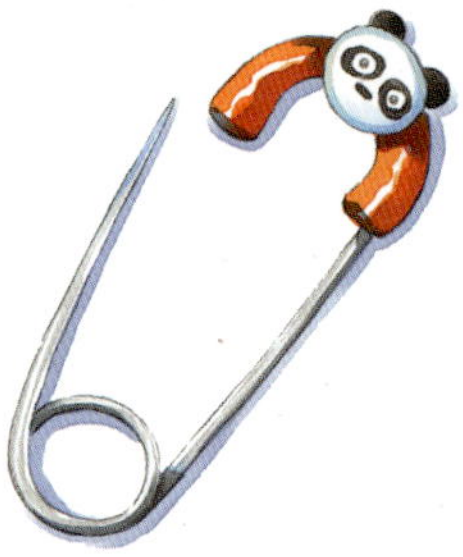

p in **pin**

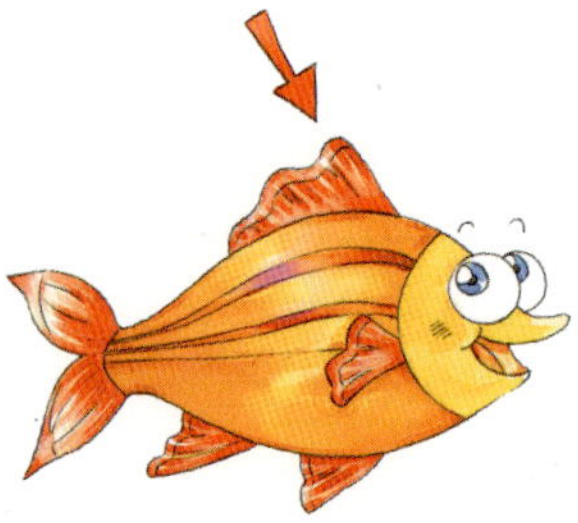

f in **fin**

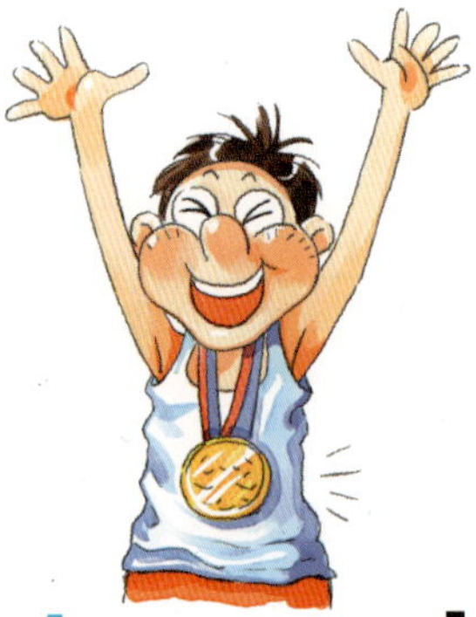

w in **win**

 Track 33

Track 34

-it

h **it** **hit**

s **it** **sit**

-id

l **id** **lid**

k **id** **kid**

Let's chant! Track 35

Read the word and circle the right picture.

1 bin 

2 hit 

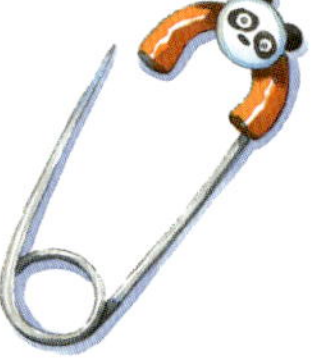 

3 kid 

4 sit 

 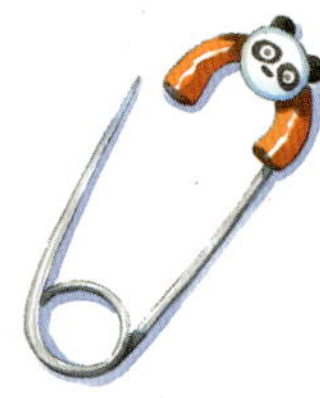

5 fin 

6 win 

Listen to the word and choose the rhyme. Then write it. 

1

in   it   id

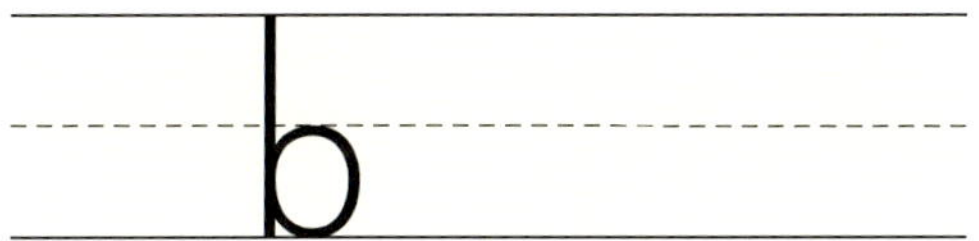

b

2

in   it   id

l

3

in   it   id

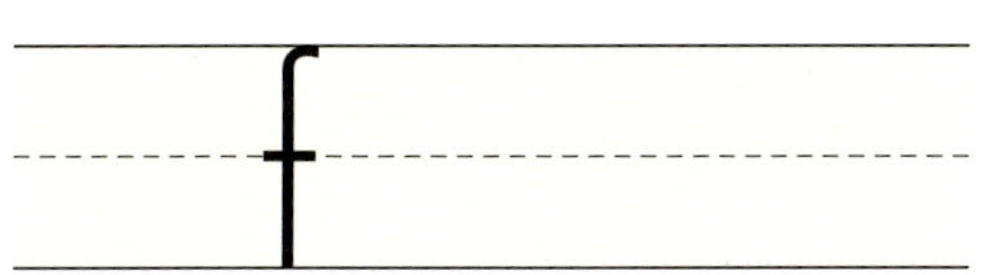

s

4

in   it   id

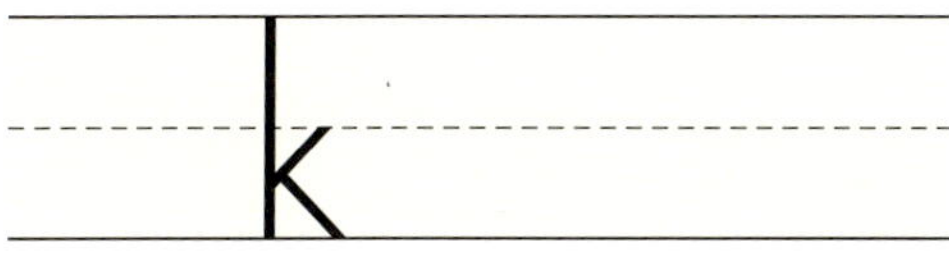

p

5

in   it   id

f

6

in   it   id

k

Listen to the word and circle the right picture. 

Listen to the word and check the right one. Track 38

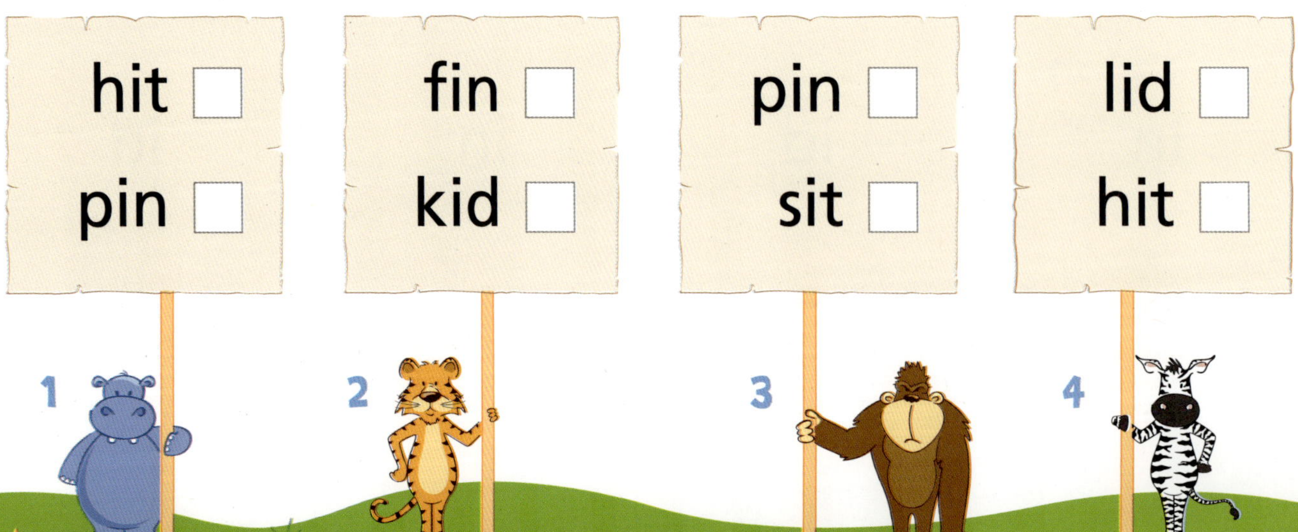

Choose and write the correct word.

1

A boy __________s on the floor.

sit	win

2

Three __________s play a game.

pin	kid

3

A fish has a long __________.

fin	lid

4

Let's __________ the baseball!

hit	bin

5

There is a __________ under the desk.

bin	kid

Who wins the race?

The fish with a fin.

The fish with a long fin wins the race.

Who hits the ball?

The kid with a pin.

The kid with a pin hits the ball.

Write the words.

-in

bin

pin

fin

win

-it

sit

hit

-id

lid

kid

Match each rhyme with right pictures.

1   **-ig** • •  • • 

2   **-ip** • •  • • 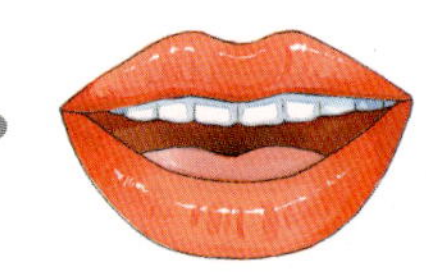

3   **-in** • •  • • 

4   **-it** • •  • • 

5   **-id** • •  • • 

Listen to the word and circle the right picture. Track 40

1

2

3

4

5

6

Listen to the word and circle the right one. Track 41

1 big   wig   dig

2 dip   rip   hip

3 fin   kid   lid

4 lip   hip   dip

5 pig   dig   big

6 bin   pin   win

Listen to the word and circle the right picture. Then write it.

1

d i p

2

h

3

k

4

p

5

b

6

w

Look at the picture and circle the right word. Then write it.

1
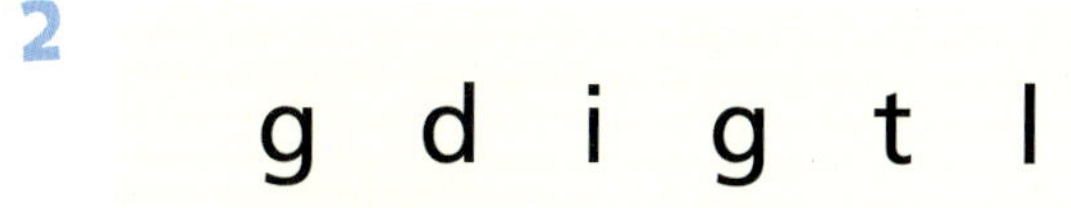

sit

2

____

3

m d w i n p

____

4

b i n f n p

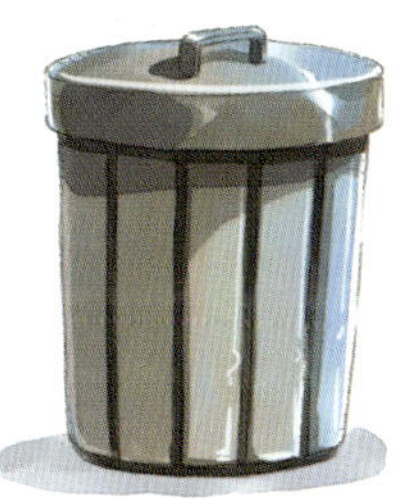

____

5
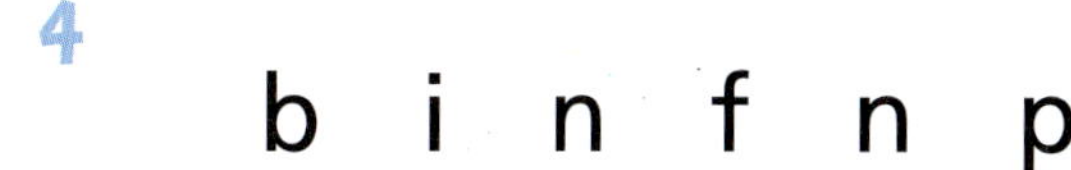

____

6
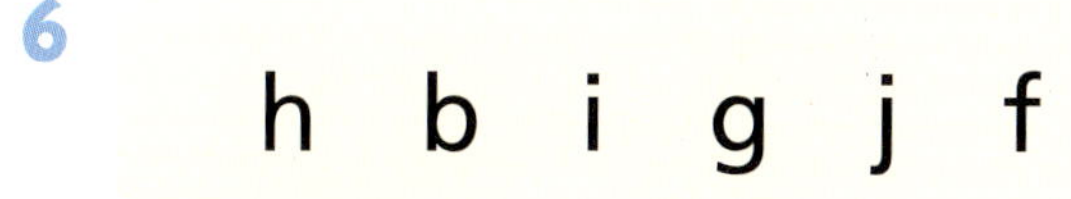

____

Unit 5 short vowel u

Listen and repeat. Track 43

u g → ug → bug

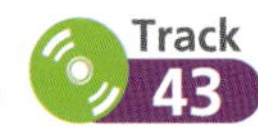

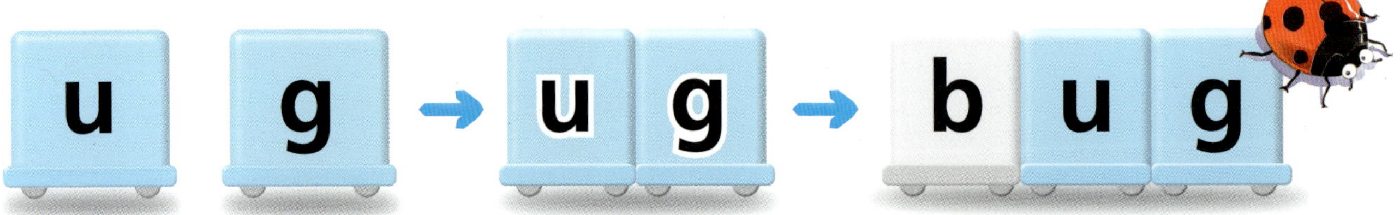

Track 44

-ug

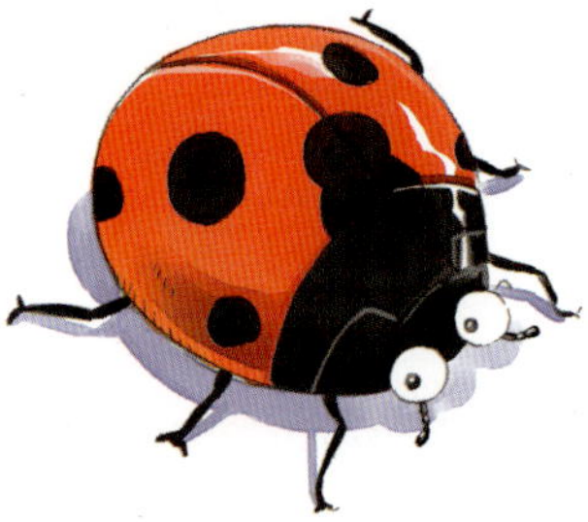

b ug **bug**

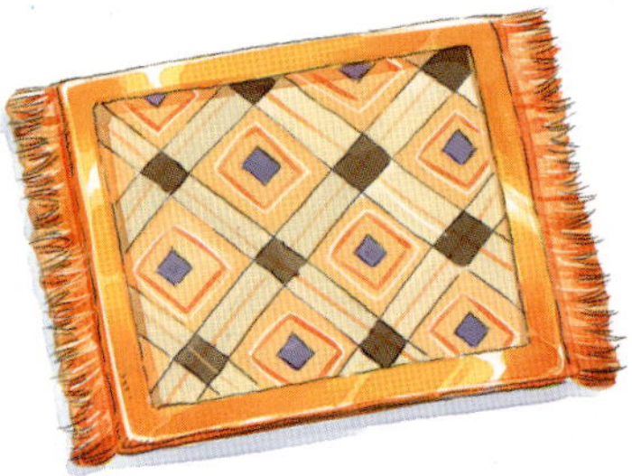

r ug **rug**

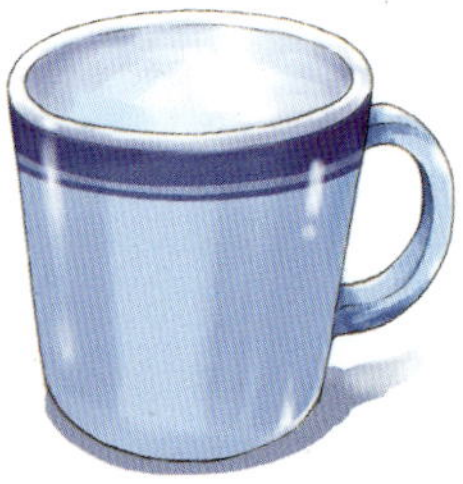

m ug **mug**

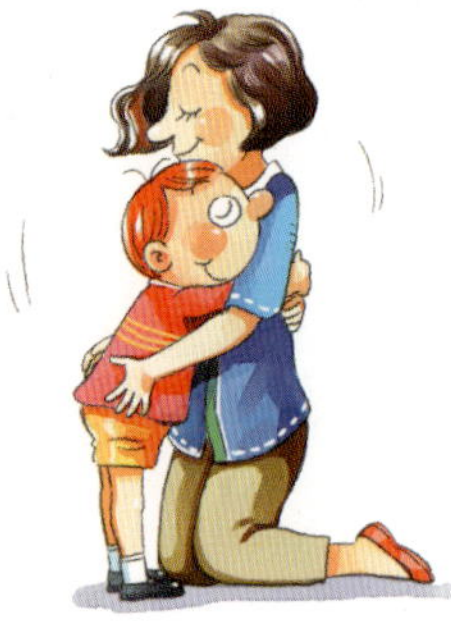

h ug **hug**

Track 46

-um

g um **gum**

dr um **drum**

-ut

n ut **nut**

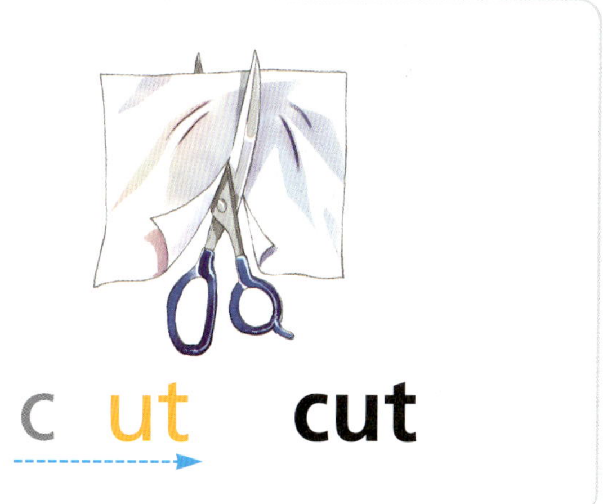

c ut **cut**

Let's chant! Track 47

Read the word and circle the right picture.

1 bug  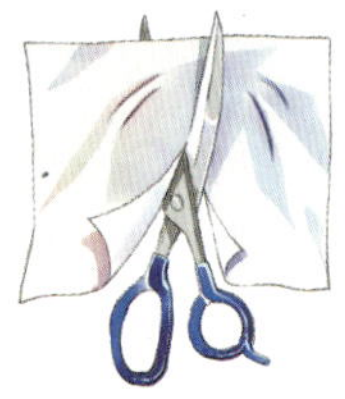 

2 mug   

3 gum   

4 nut   

5 drum   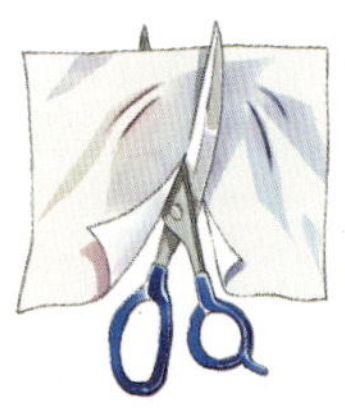

6 cut  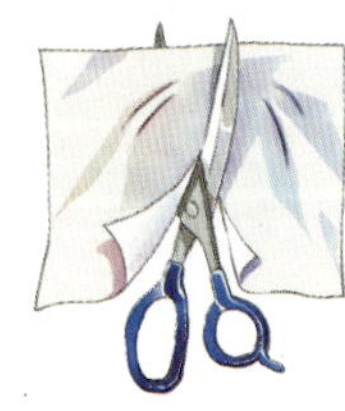 

Listen to the word and match the rhyme. Then write it. 

1 

2 

-ug

m

h

3 

-um

g

dr

4 

5 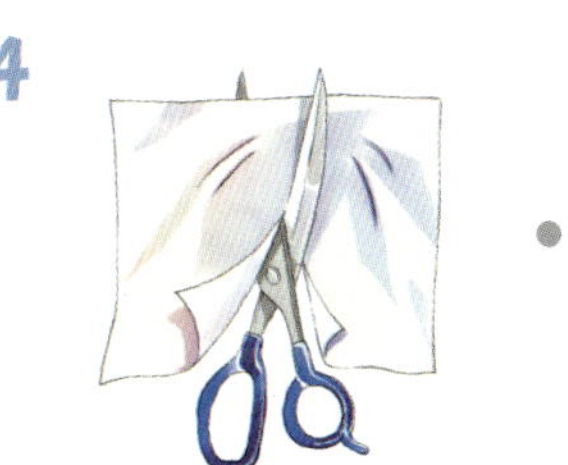

-ut

n

c

6 

Listen to the word and circle the right picture. 

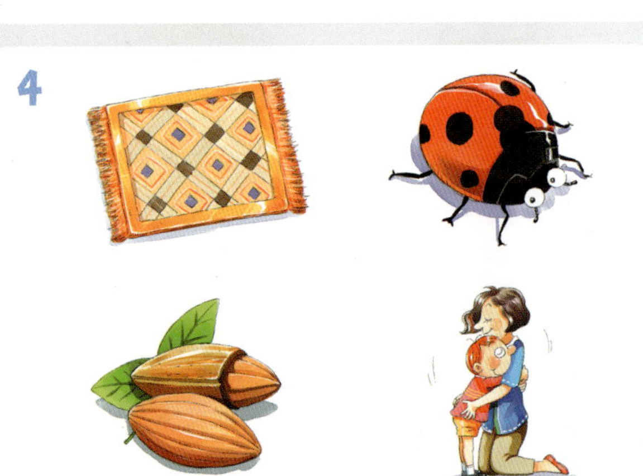

Listen to the word and check the right one.

Choose and write the correct word.

1

Kate __________s her dog.

| nut | hug |

2

A girl plays the __________.

| rug | drum |

3

The milk is in the __________.

| mug | nut |

4

A bug eats a __________.

| nut | gum |

5

A boy __________s the paper.

| mug | cut |

Read Along!

Six bugs fly in the room.

Two bugs drink milk from a mug.

Two bugs chew gum on a drum.

Two bugs cut and eat the nuts on a rug.

Now six bugs hug and dance.

Write the words.

-ug

bug

rug

mug

hug

-um

gum

drum

-ut

nut

cut

Unit 6

short vowel u

Listen and repeat. Track 52

u n → un → sun

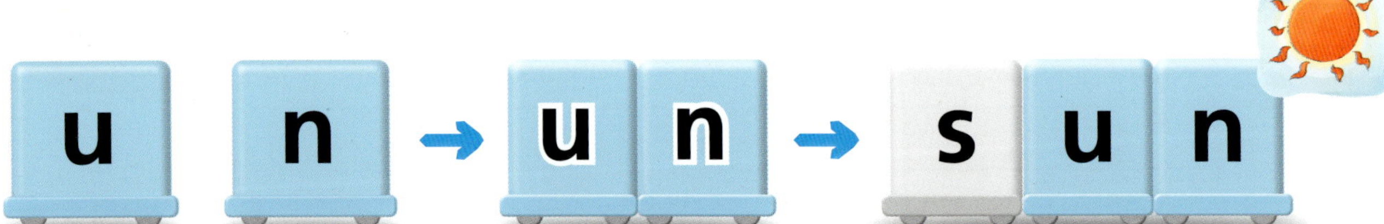

Track 53

-un

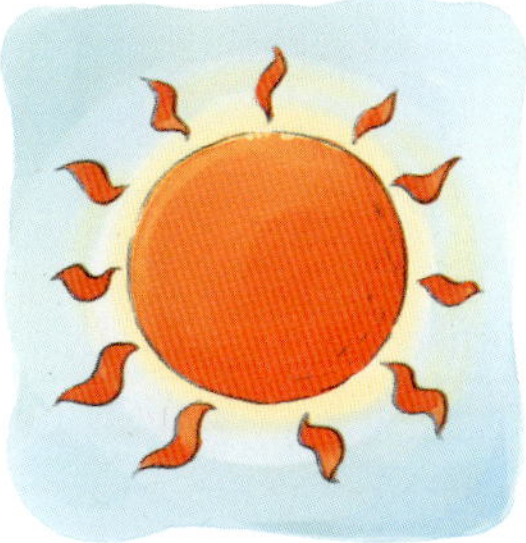

s un sun

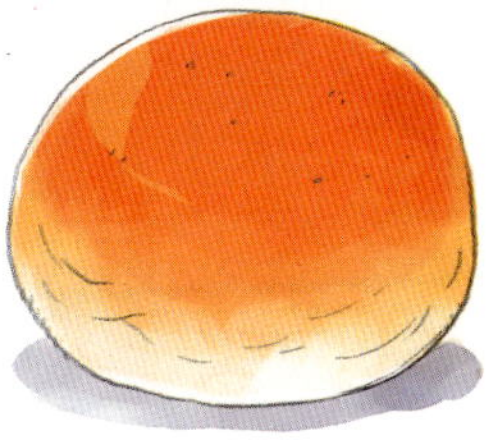

b un bun

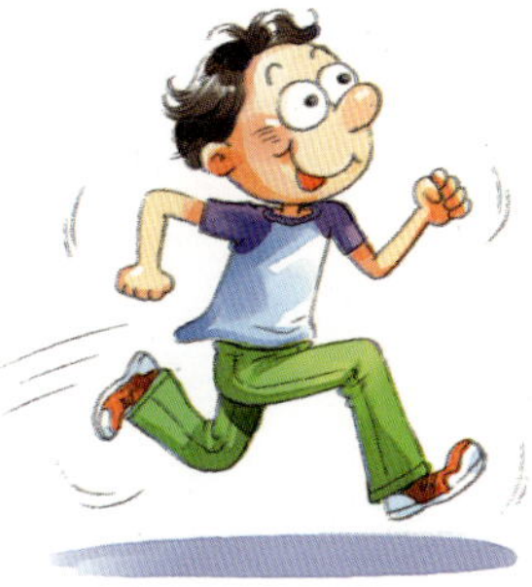

r un run

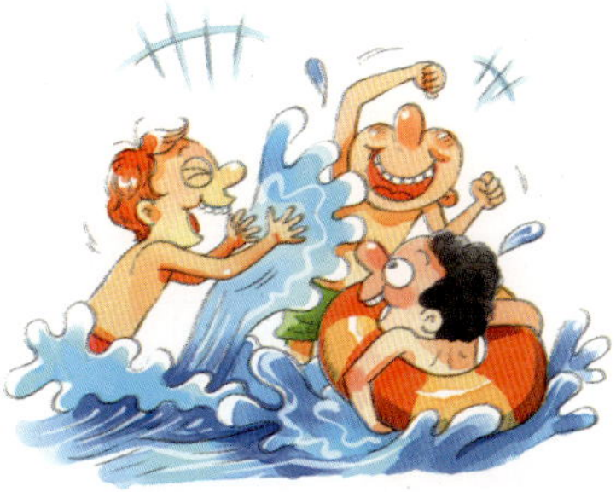

f un fun

Track 55

-ub

c ub **cub**

t ub **tub**

-ud

m ud **mud**

b ud **bud**

Let's chant! Track 56

Read the word and circle the right picture.

1 sun

 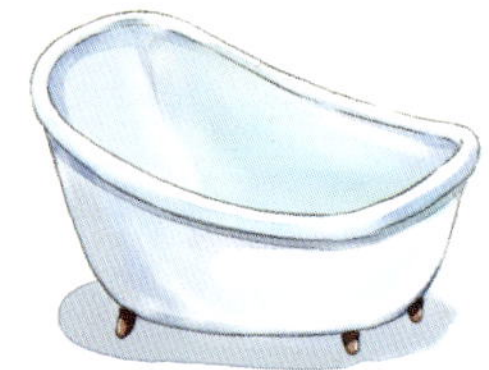 

2 run

3 cub

4 tub

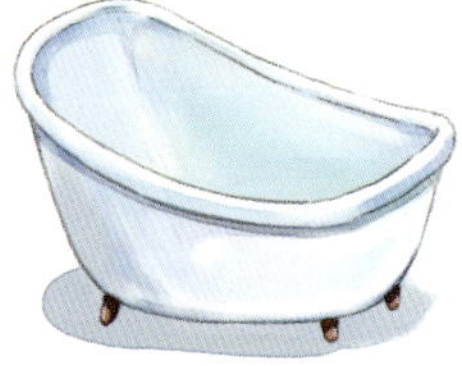  

5 bud

6 mud

  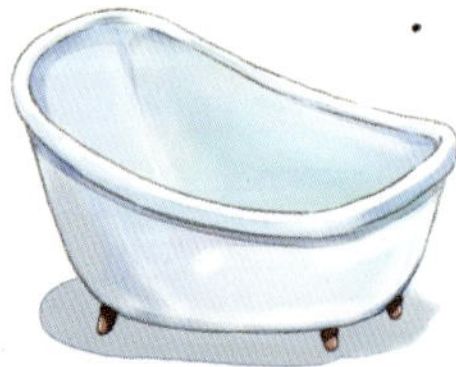

Listen to the word and match the rhyme. Then write it. 

1

r

f

-un

2

3

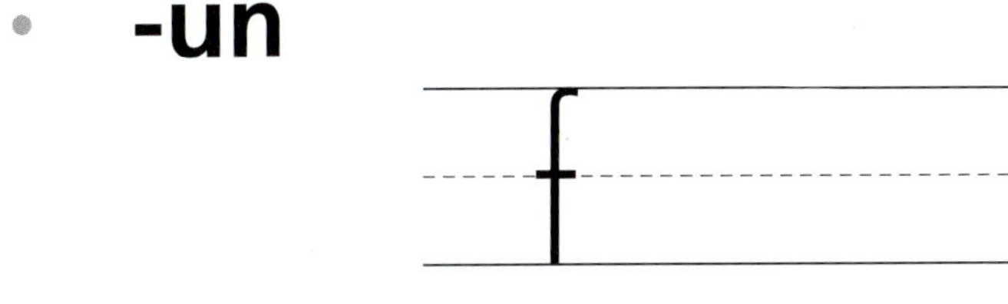

m

b

-ud

4

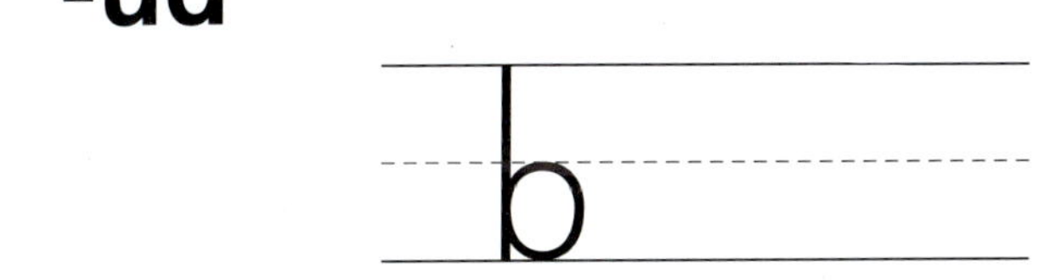

5

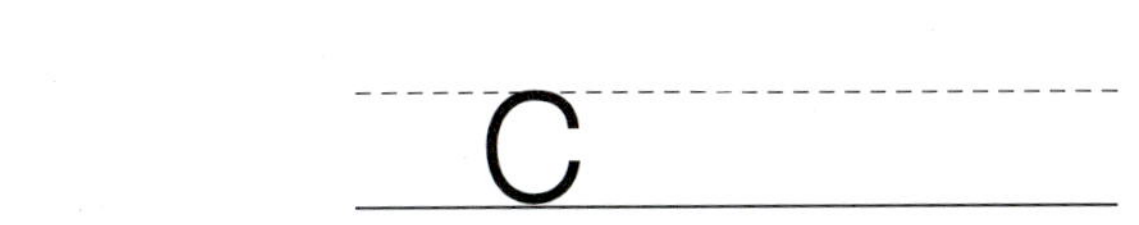

c

t

-ub

6

Listen to the word and circle the right picture. 

Listen to the word and check the right one.

bun ☐	mud ☐	run ☐	fun ☐
bud ☐	cub ☐	tub ☐	bud ☐
1	2	3	4

Choose and write the correct word.

1

A ___________ plays with a ball.

| bud | cub |

2

The ___________ is in the sky.

| sun | mud |

3

Children ___________ on the street.

| run | tub |

4

A boy plays with the ___________.

| bun | mud |

5

A girl is in the ___________.

| tub | bun |

A little cub plays with the mud.
Looks fun! Looks fun!
"Oh! You are dirty!"

Take a bath in the tub.
Looks clean! Looks clean!
"Oh! You are clean!"

Come and have some buns.
Smells good! Smells good!
"Oh! It smells good!"

Write the words.

-un

sun

bun

run

fun

-ub

cub

tub

-ud

mud

bud

Circle the rhyme for each picture and write the word.

1

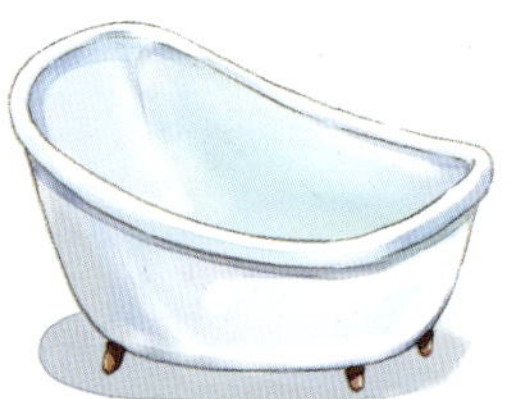

ug
un
ud

_r_______

2

um
ug
ub

_t_______

3

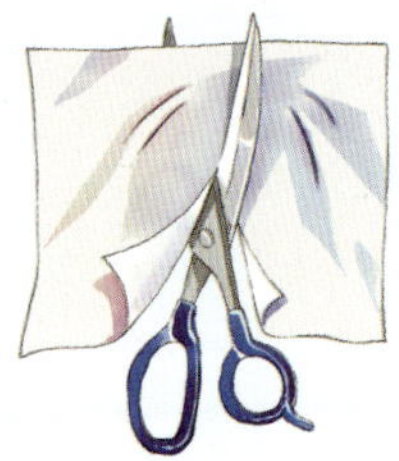

ud
ut
um

_c_______

4

ug
ub
un

_r_______

5

ud
ug
ub

_b_______

6

um
ub
ug

_m_______

Listen to the word and circle the right one. Then match the right picture. **Track 61**

1
rug
mug

2
cut
nut

3
fun
run

4
bug
hug

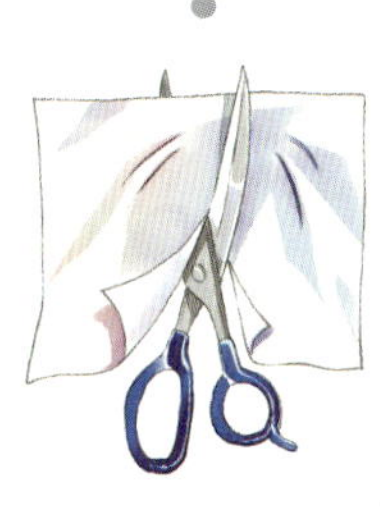

5
sun
bun

6
cut
cub

7
gum
drum

8
bud
mud

Listen to the word and write it. Then match the right picture.

1 c u b

2 _ n _

3 _ b _

4 _ h _

5 _ f _

6 _ m _

Find the given words in the puzzle. Then write each word under the right picture.

Words rug drum mug tub cub sun

r	u	g	m	a	g
t	d	r	u	m	n
s	e	l	g	u	v
t	f	i	d	q	w
u	c	u	b	y	x
b	a	g	s	u	n

1

____

2

____

3

____

4

____

5

____

6

____

short vowel o

Listen and repeat. **Track 63**

Track 64

-og

l og **log**

j og **jog**

-op

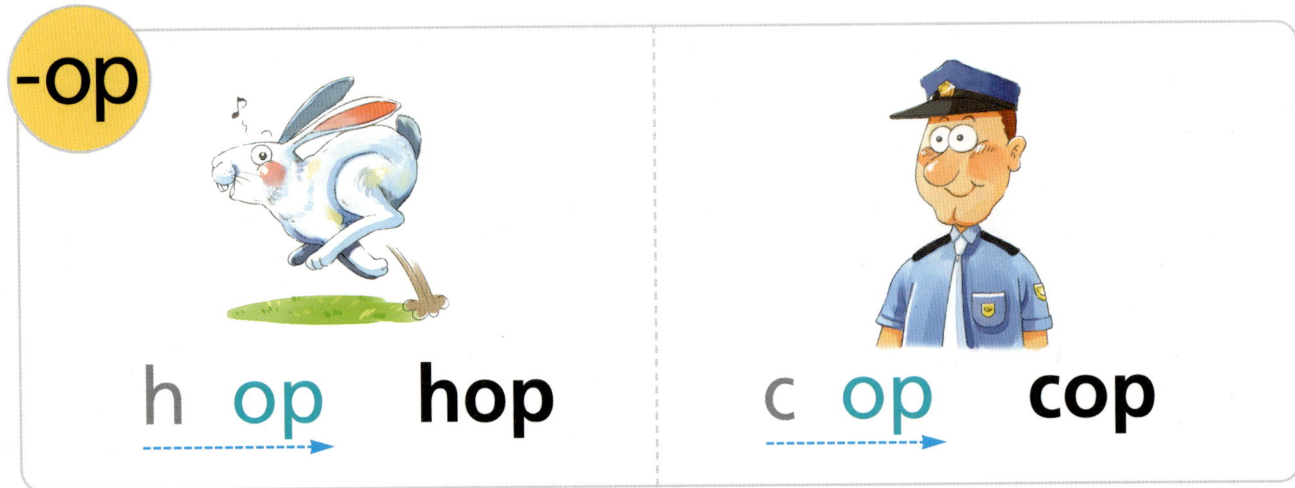

h op **hop**

c op **cop**

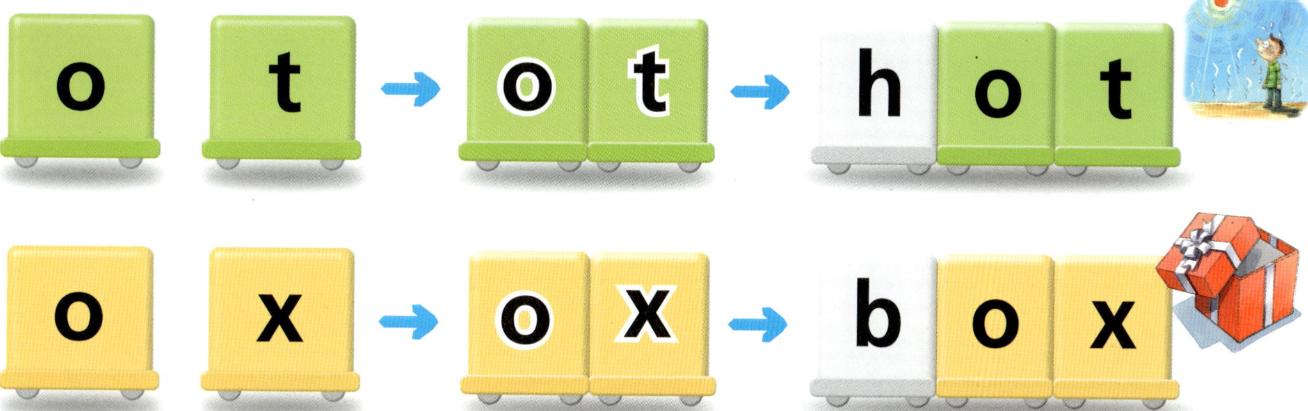

Track 66

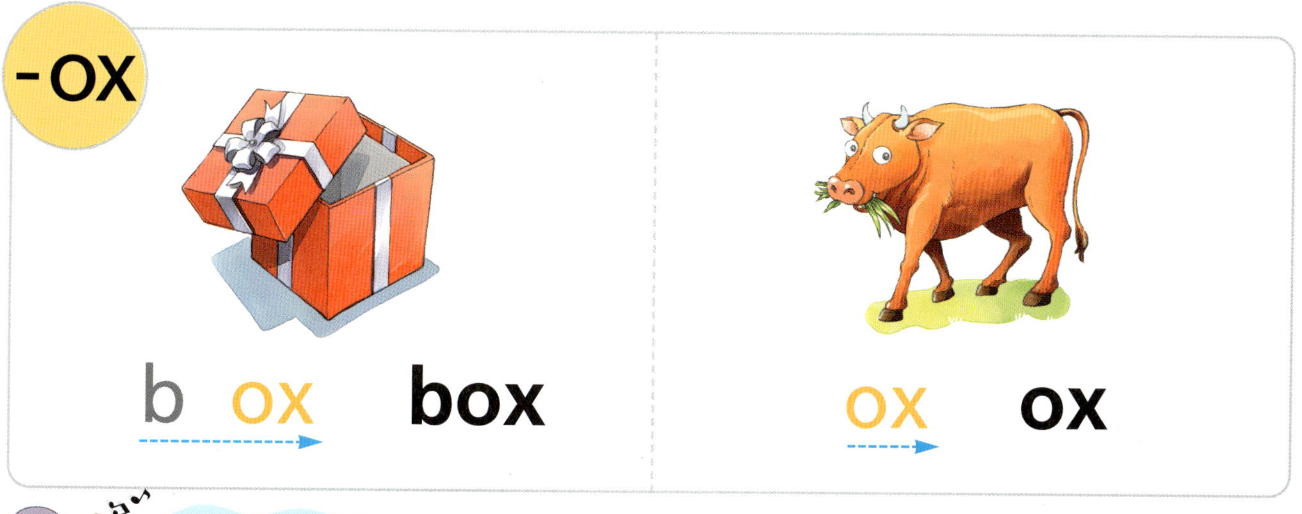

Let's chant! Track 67

Read the word and circle the right picture.

1 jog

2 ox

3 log

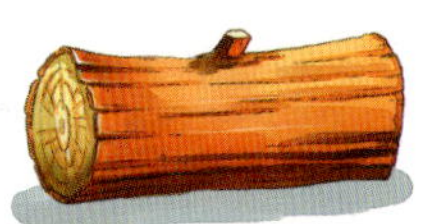  

4 cop

5 dot

6 box

Listen to the word and match the rhyme. Then write it.

1

2

c

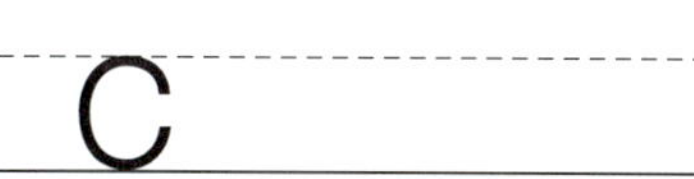

3

h

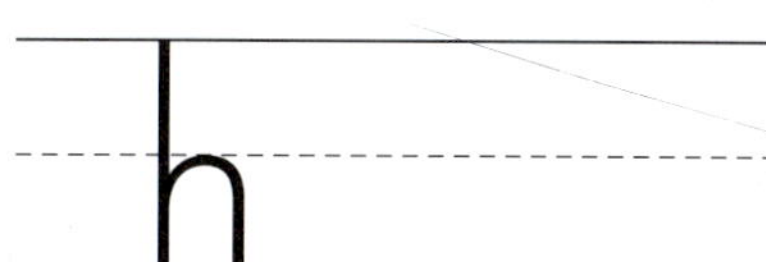

4

d

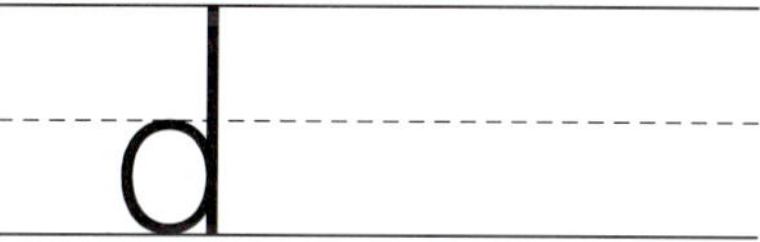

5

h

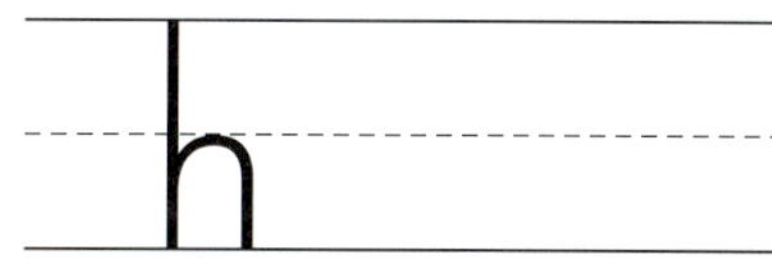

6

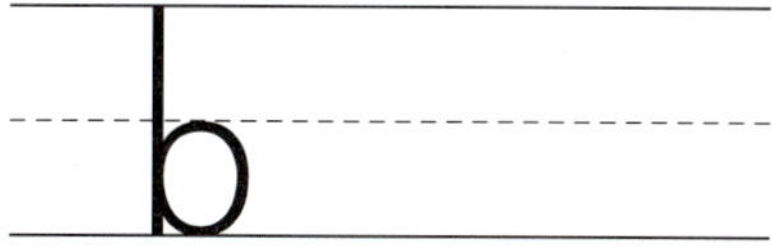

b

Listen to the word and circle the right picture. 

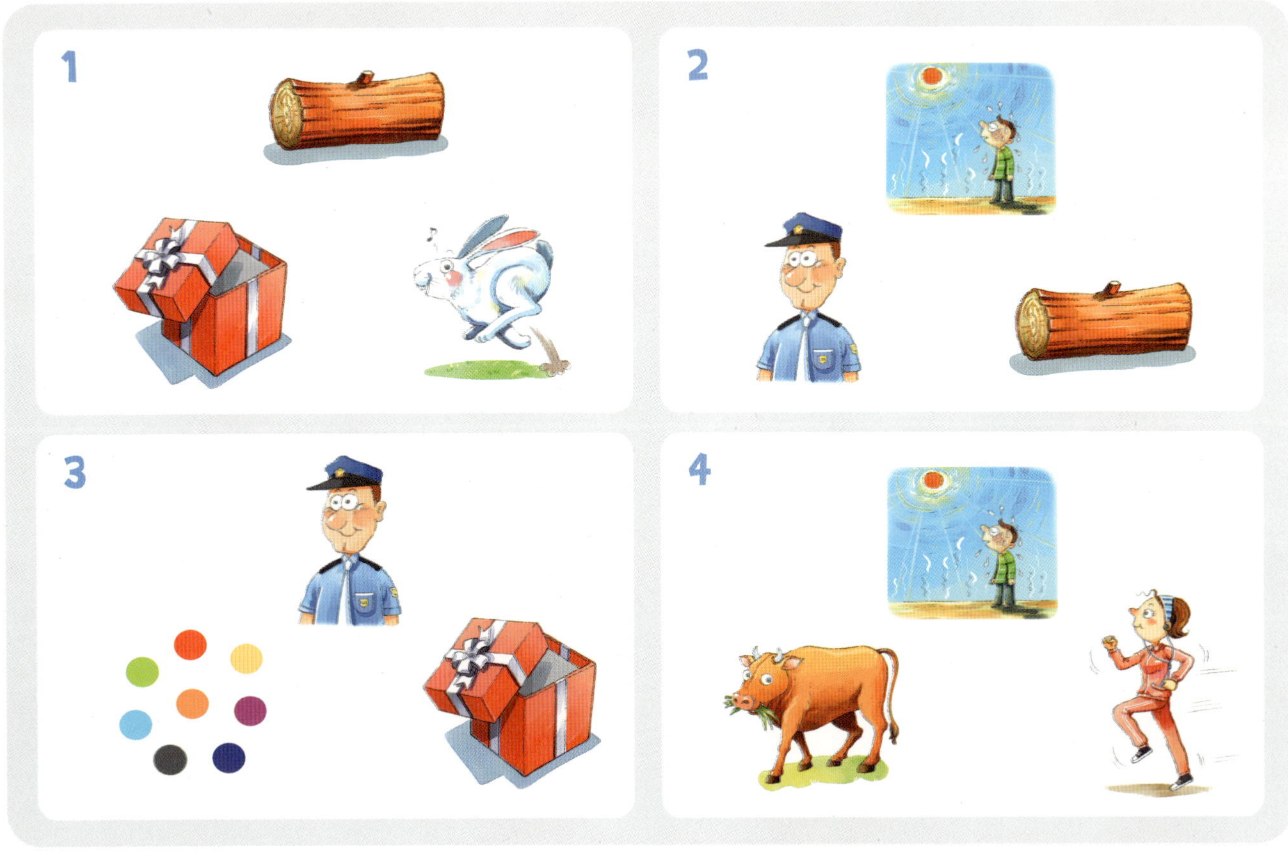

Listen to the word and check the right one.

Choose and write the correct word.

1 

A cat is in the _____________.

| log | box |

2 

The pan is ___________.

| hot | cop |

3 

A girl __________s on the ground.

| jog | hop |

4 

A ___________ is beside the car.

| dot | cop |

5 

There are many __________s on
the blouse.

| log | dot |

Read Along!

The cop goes for a jog.

He jumps over the log.

It's hot! It's hot!

The ox hops and hops.

He hops into the box.

He's hot! He's hot!

Write the words.

-og
jog

log

-op
hop

cop

-ot
hot

dot

-ox
box

ox

short vowel e

Listen and repeat. Track 72

e d → e d → b e d

e t → e t → n e t

Track 73

-ed

b ed **bed**

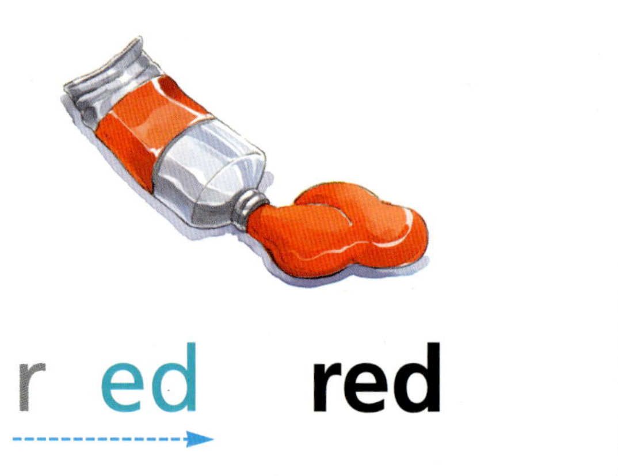

r ed **red**

-et

n et **net**

p et **pet**

Track 75

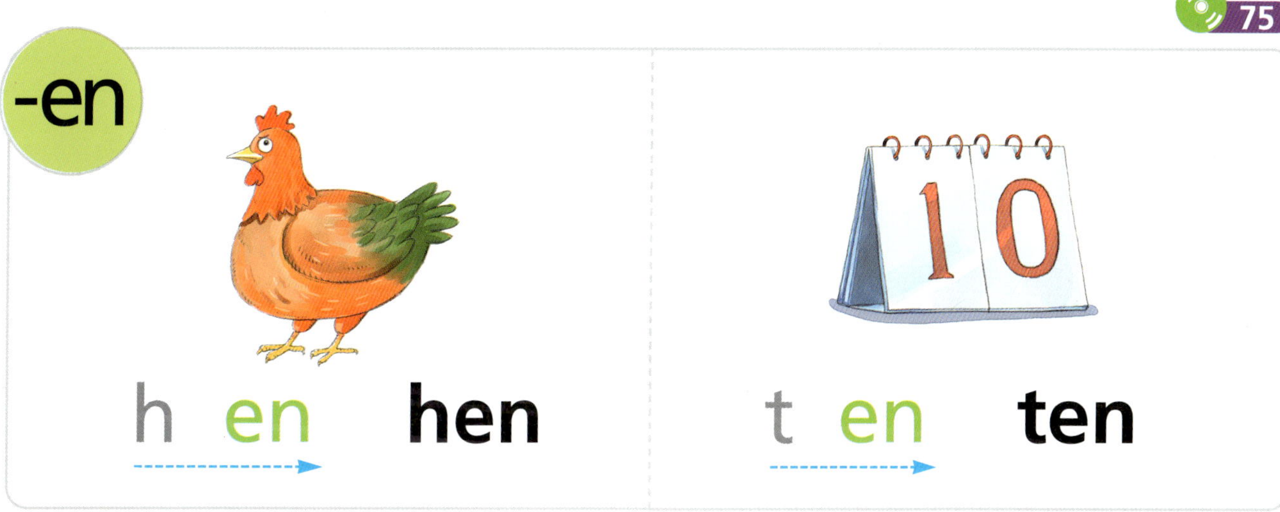

-en

h en **hen**

t en **ten**

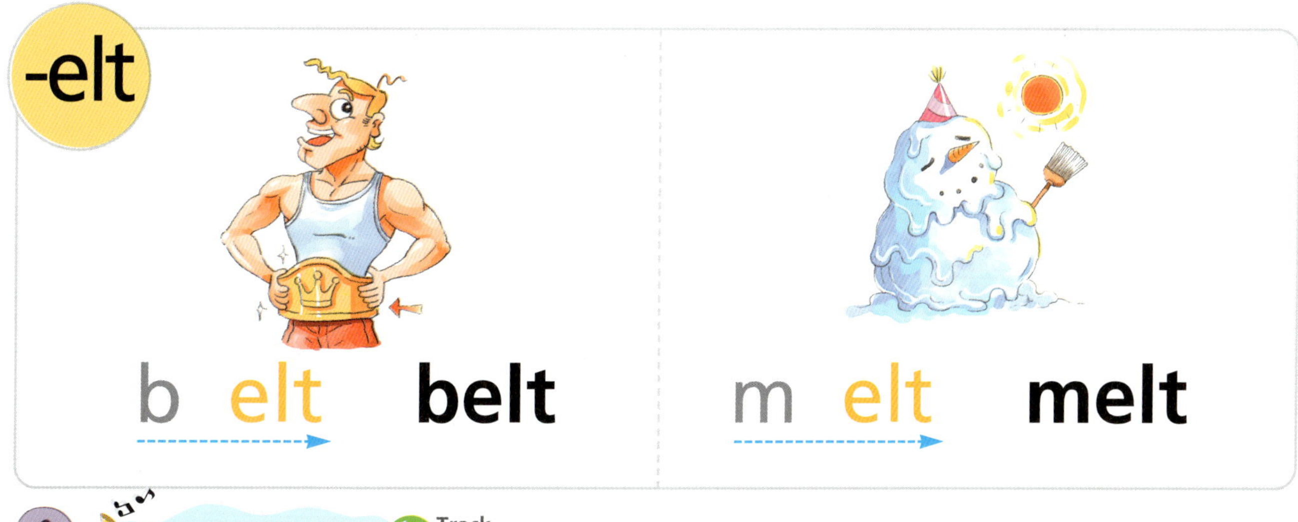

-elt

b elt **belt**

m elt **melt**

Read the word and circle the right picture.

1 bed

2 hen

3 red

4 net

5 ten

6 pet

1

-ed

2

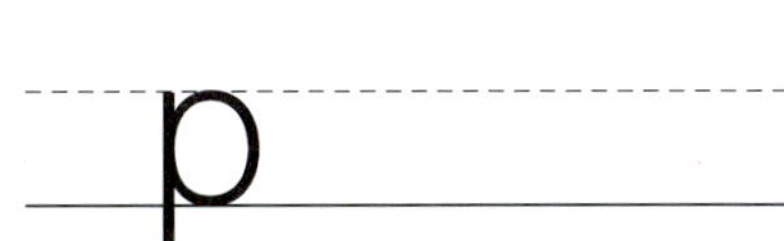

3

-et

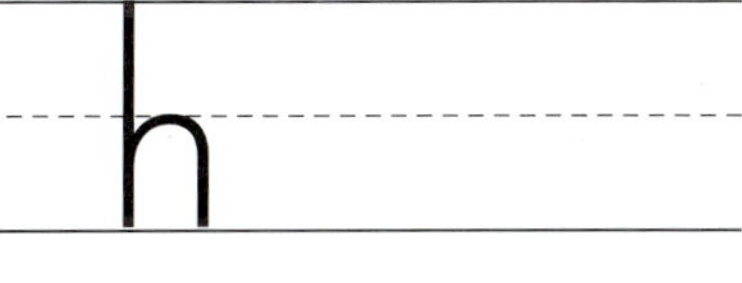

4

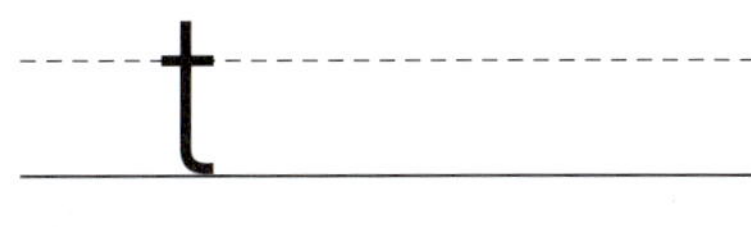

-en

5

6

-elt

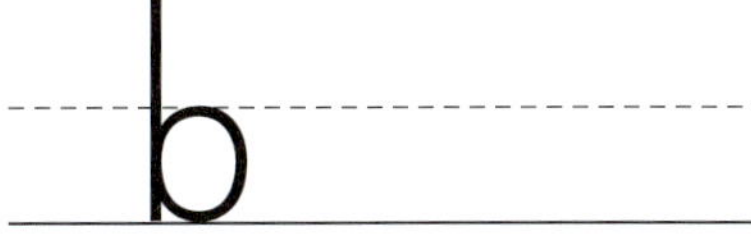

Track 78

Listen to the word and check the right one.

Track 79

Choose and write the correct word.

1

A dog is on the __________.

bed | belt

2

A __________ eats a bug.

hen | red

3

A boy wears a blue __________.

belt | pet

4

Cindy likes her __________ skirt.

net | red

5

The ice __________s on the hand.

melt | belt

I'm Jen. I'm ten.

I need a new bed.

"Can I have a net for a bed?"
"No, you will fall," says Mom.

"Can I have an igloo for a bed?"
"No, it will melt," says Dad.

"How about this red bed?" says Grandma.

Yes, I love my new red bed!

Write the words.

-ed

bed

red

-et

net

pet

-en

hen

ten

-elt

belt

melt

Match the picture to the right rhyme and write the word.

1

- -og
- -et

n _______

2

- -ot
- -ed

h _______

3

- -ox
- -en

b _______

4

- -op
- -ed

r _______

5

- -ot
- -elt

b _______

6

- -og
- -en

l _______

Listen to the word and circle the right one. Then match the right picture. Track 81

1 log / jog

2 bed / red

3 pet / net

4 hen / ten

5 hop / cop

6 ox / box

7 belt / melt

8 dot / hot

Listen to the word and match the letter to the right rhyme. Then write the word.

1 l   o g   b   e g

____

2 h   e t   n   o t

____

3 j   e n   h   e t

____

4 b   e lt   h   o p

____

5 r   o t   d   e d

____

6 c   o p   b   o x

____

Look at the picture and write the word in the puzzle.

1

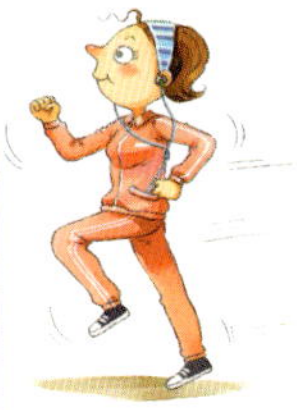

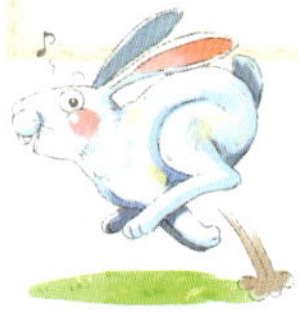

①

②

j

o

g

2

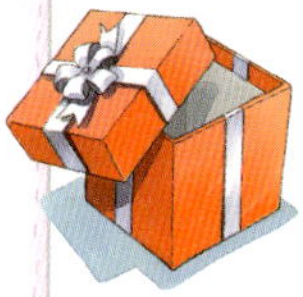

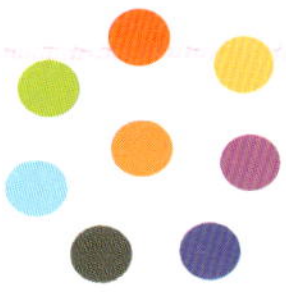

①

②

3

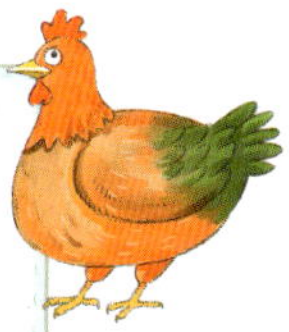

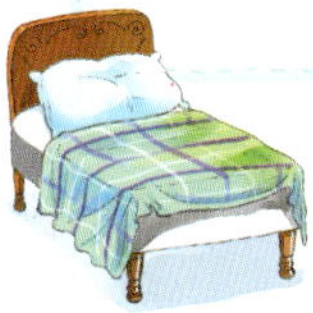

①

②

4

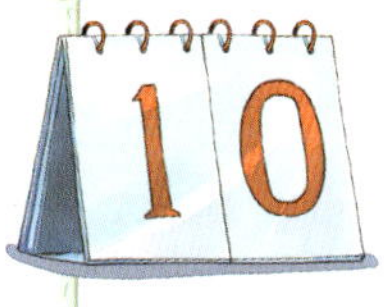

①

②

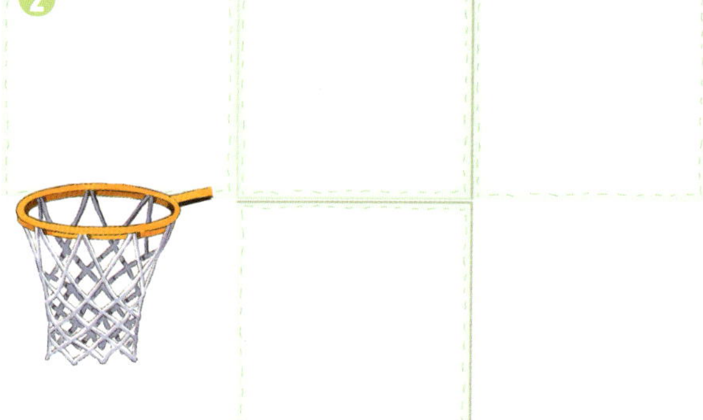

Final Review

Circle the correct word for the picture. Then write it.

1 

fan   pan

2 

pig   wig

3 

melt   belt

4 

dot   dog

5 

bun   run

6 

hen   ten

7 

hat   mat

8 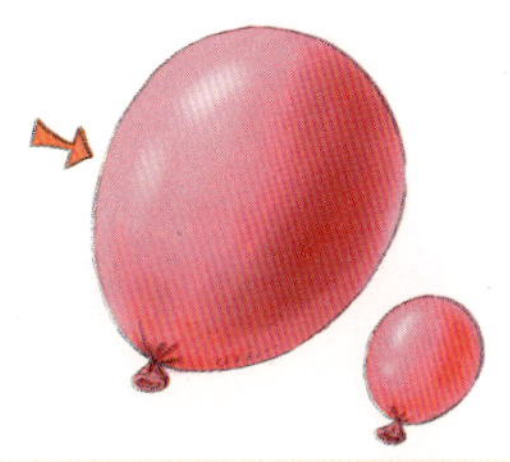

big   bug

9 

fin   pin

Judy wants to buy a present for her sister. Listen to the word and circle the right picture. Track 83

Q. What did Judy buy for her sister?

A. A red ___ ___ ___ .

1 b__g	**2** d__g	**3** k__d
4 h__g	**5** c__p	**6** b__lt
7 t__p	**8** c__n	**9** l__p
10 c__t	**11** m__d	**12** r__d

Choose and write the correct word for the picture.

1

The sofa is blue and the __________ is __________ .

| bag | red |

2

Tom __________s every morning.
He runs with his __________ .

| pet | jog |

3

A girl drops a __________ .
She looks so __________ .

| sad | mug |

4

A __________ is on the __________ .
He eats some __________s.

| pig | rug | bun |

Let's read the story.

Check the pictures, referring to the words from the story.

3

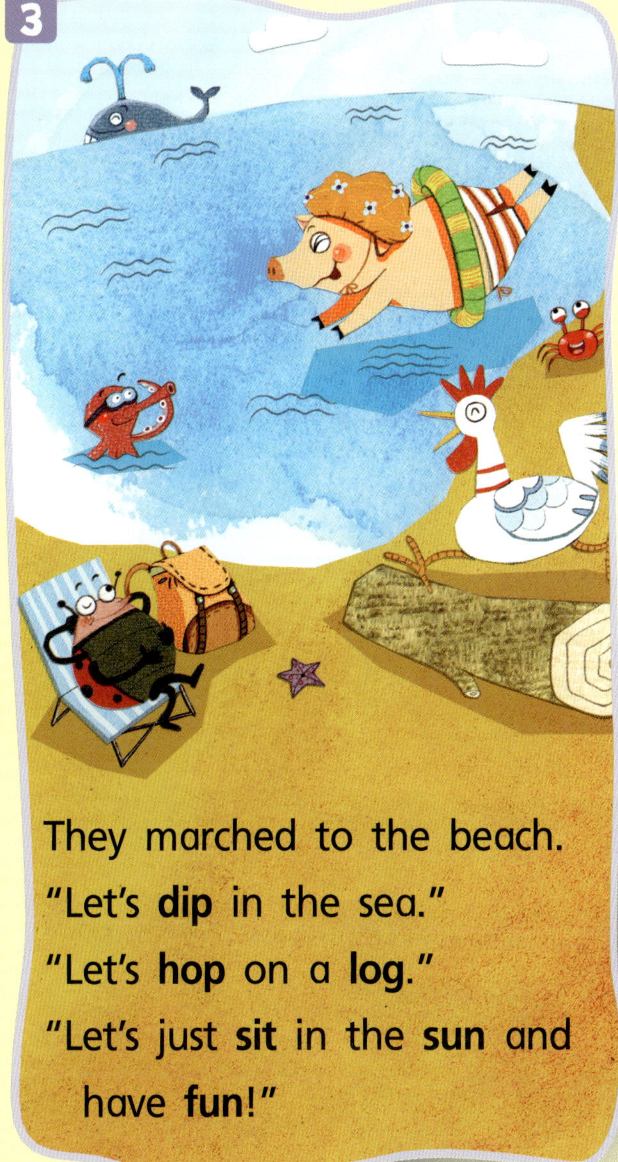

They marched to the beach.
"Let's **dip** in the sea."
"Let's **hop** on a **log**."
"Let's just **sit** in the **sun** and have **fun**!"

4

"Now it's too **hot**!" said the Hen.
"We are too **red**!" said the Pig.
"It's time to go home," said the Bug.

Let's play a game.
Start!
-en
-ed
-ot
-ub
-at
-an
-og
-am
-un
-ap
-op
-ud
-ag
-elt
-ad
-am
-in
-ut
-ig
-um
-ox
-ap
TICKETS

How to play
Step 1 Roll a dice with your friend.
Step 2 Say a word with the given rhyme.
Step 3 If you get to the "End!" first, you will win this game.
-in
-ip
-op
-ox
-un
-ug
-id
-it
-ip
-et
-um
-ag
-ed
-elt
-ig
-ap
-ud
-ot
-in
-et
-it
End!

Final Test

Listen to the word and check the right number. 

e.g.

 ✔ ① jog ② pig ③ bug

1

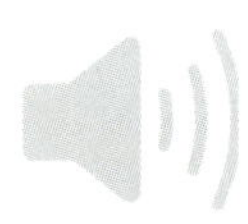 ① hit ② hen ③ melt

2

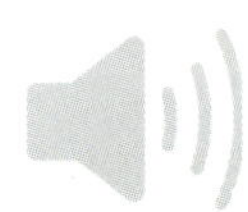 ① sad ② sit ③ sun

3

 ① hip ② lip ③ log

4

 ① dad ② bed ③ mat

5

 ① rip ② tub ③ lap

Listen to the word and check the right number. 

e.g.  ①     ②     ③  

6  ①    ② 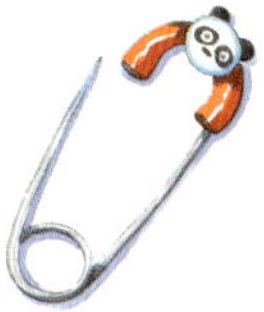   ③ 

7  ①    ②    ③ 

8  ①    ②    ③ 

9  ①    ②    ③ 

10  ①    ②    ③ 

Listen to the word and check the right number with the given ending rhyme. **Track 88**

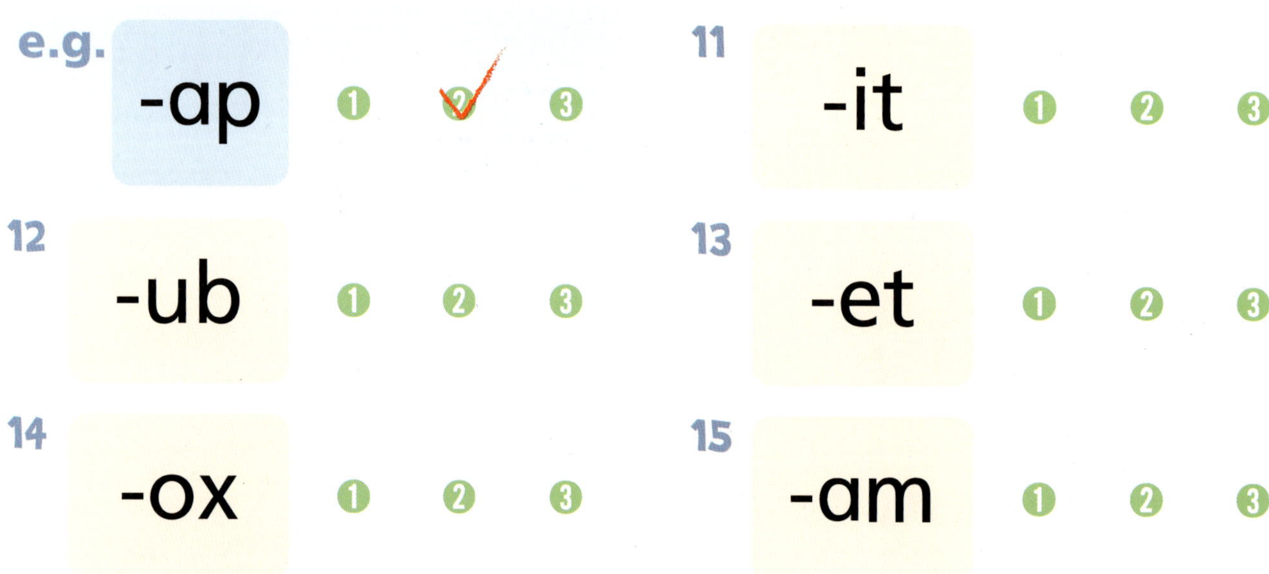

e.g.
-ap ① ✓② ③

11 -it ① ② ③

12 -ub ① ② ③

13 -et ① ② ③

14 -ox ① ② ③

15 -am ① ② ③

Listen to the word and choose the rhyme. Then write it.  **Track 89**

e.g.
-an
-at
h a t

16
-ad
-it
s _ _

17
-ig
-in
w _ _

18
-in
-um
dr _ _

19
-ug
-ud
b _ _

20
-un
-in
b _ _

Check the picture with the different rhyme.

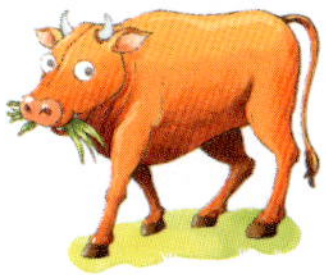

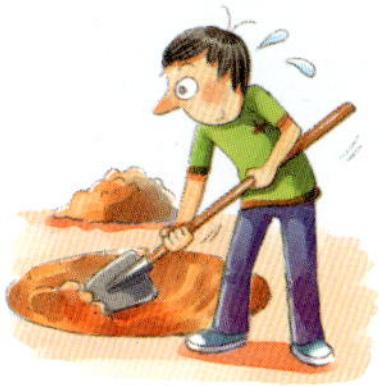

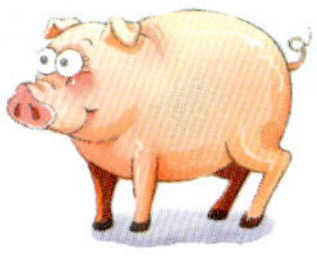

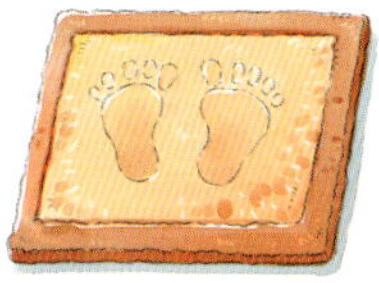

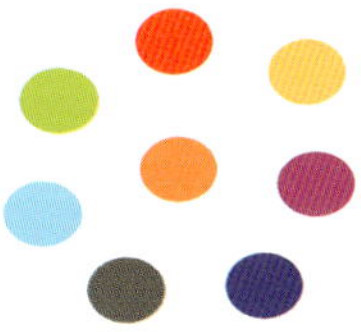

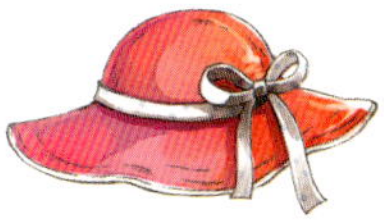

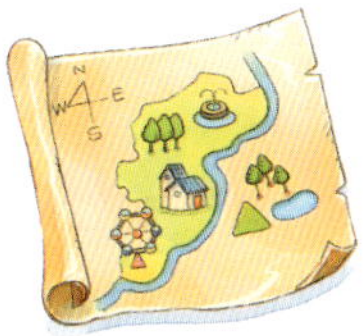

e.g.

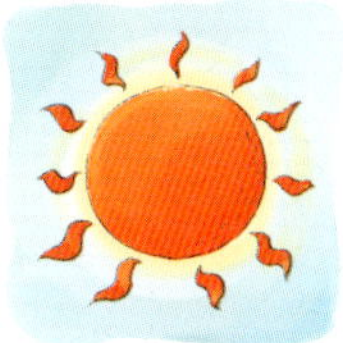

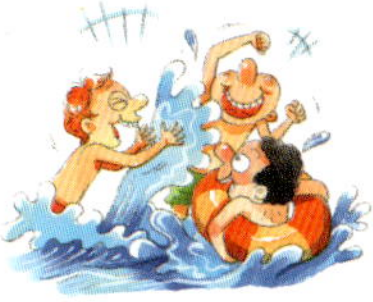

21

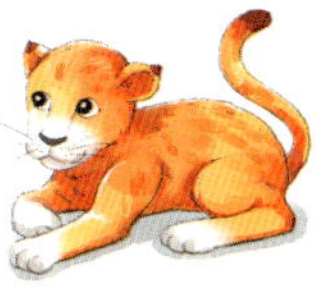

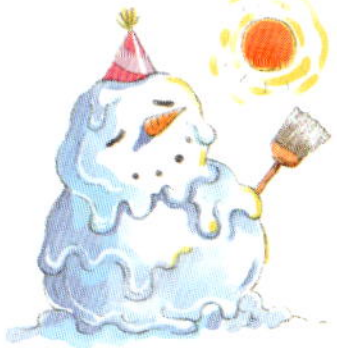

22

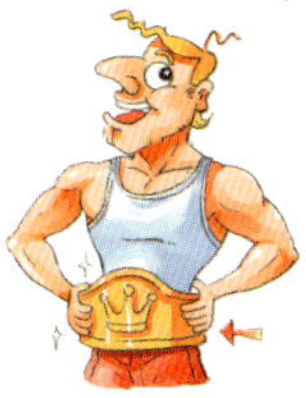

23

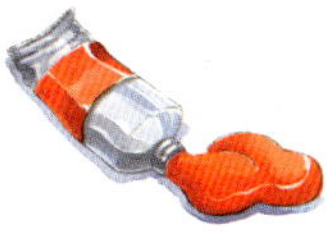

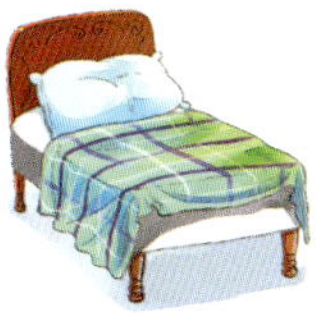

24

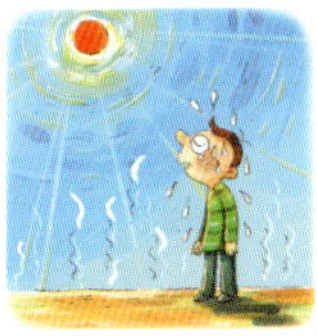

25

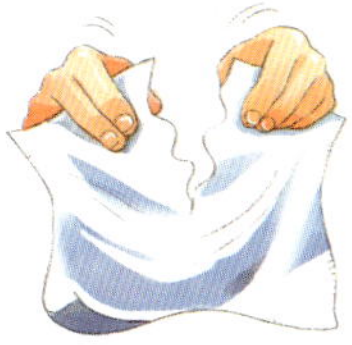

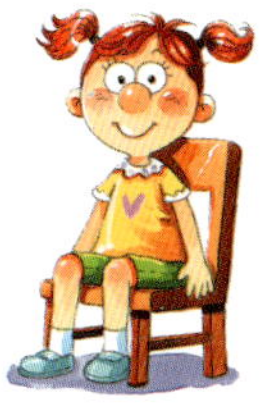

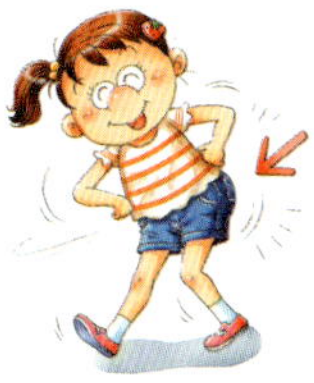

Write the correct word for the picture.

e.g.

ten

26

27

28

29

30

31

32

Look at the picture and choose the correct word. Then write it.

e.g.

A man wears a __hat__ and holds a __box__.

can	hat	box	log

33

A ________ fish is in the ________.

hot	big	mud	gum

34

A boy ________s on the ________.

sit	bin	pan	fan

35

Dad wears a ________ and ________s in the park.

mat	cap	hop	jog

36

A girl ________s a big ________ in her arms.

hug	run	pig	pin

Glossary

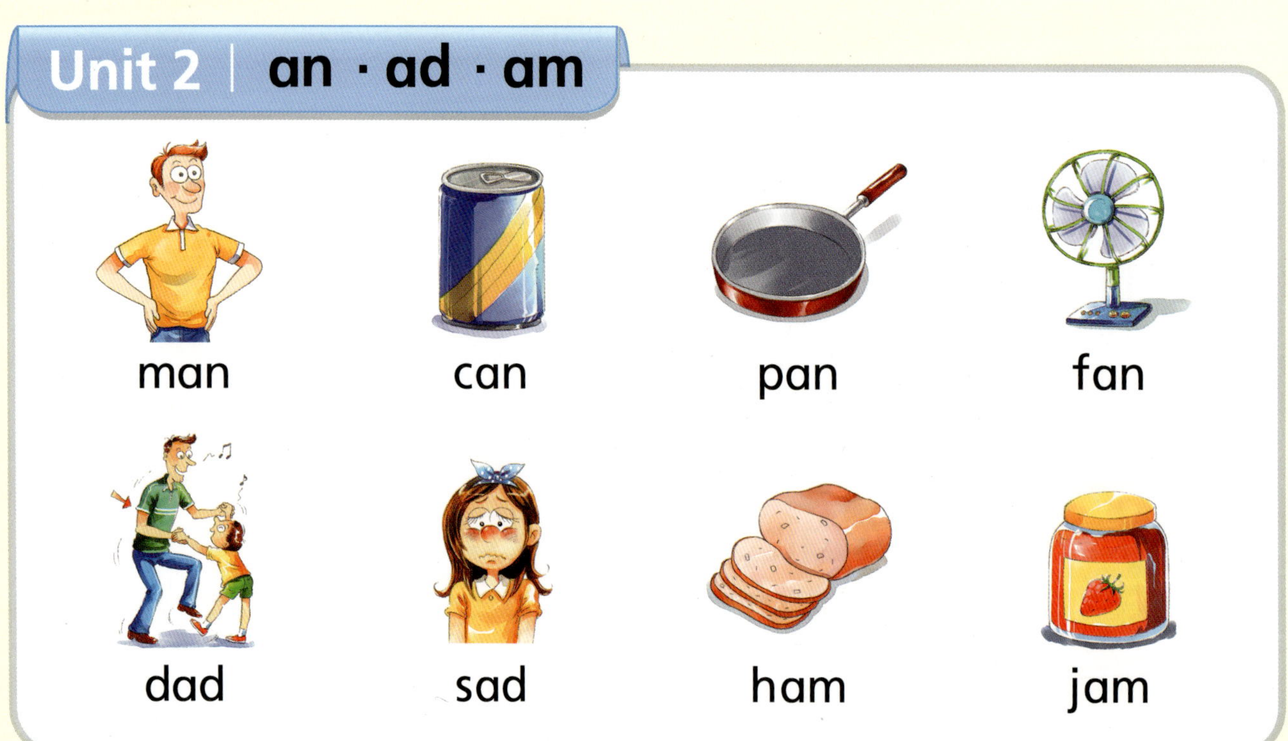

Unit 3 | ig · ip

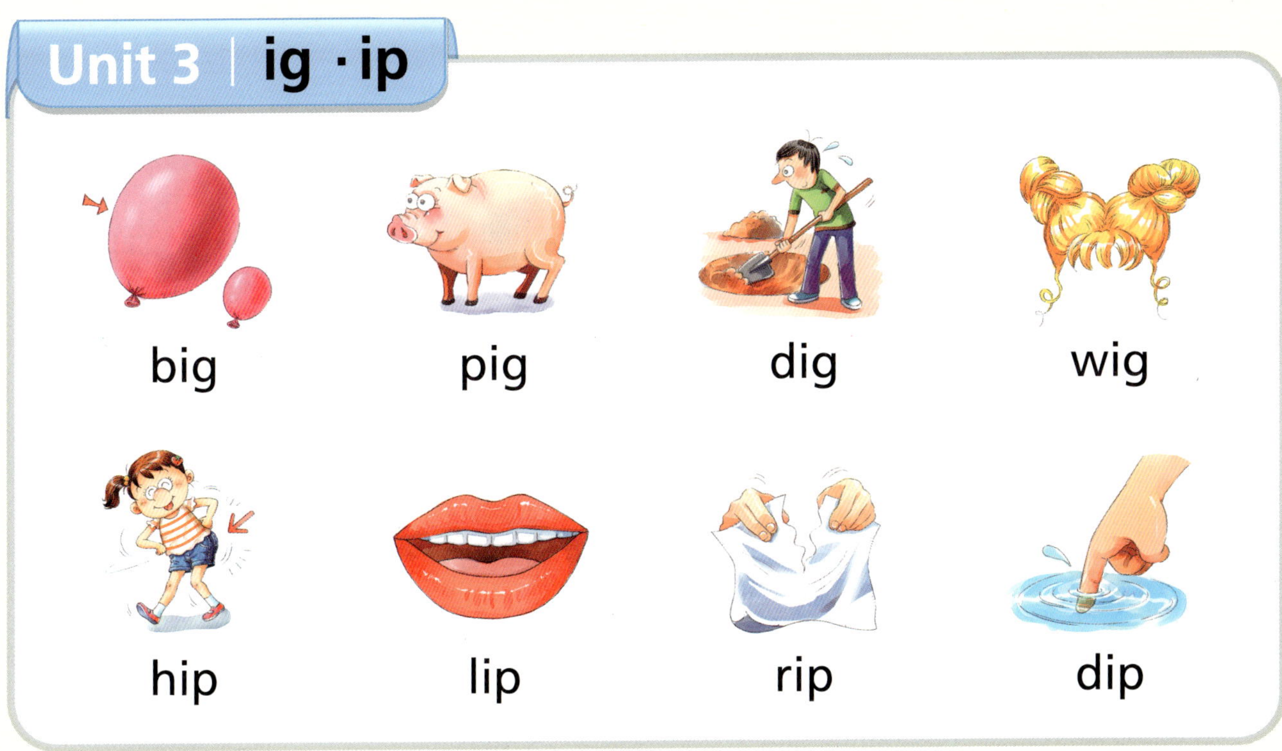

big · pig · dig · wig

hip · lip · rip · dip

Unit 4 | in · it · id

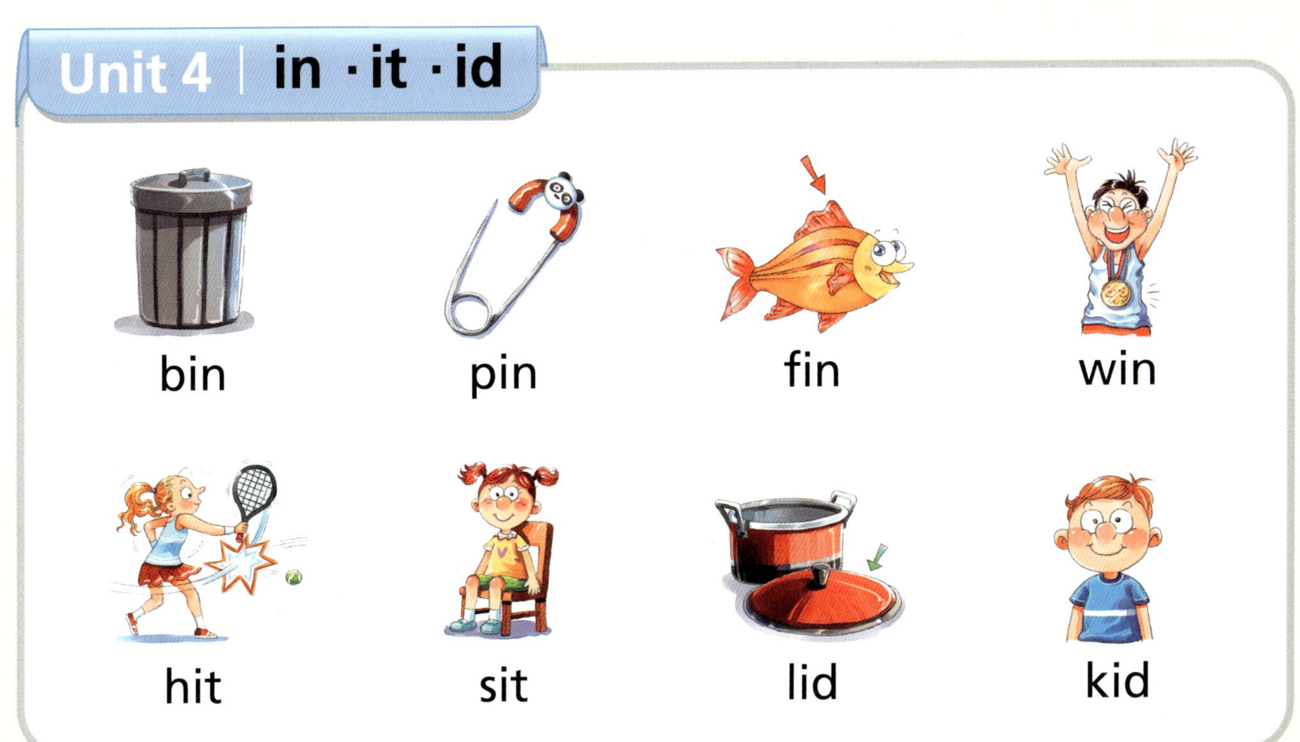

bin · pin · fin · win

hit · sit · lid · kid

Glossary

Unit 5 | ug · um · ut

bug   rug   mug   hug

gum   drum   nut   cut

Unit 6 | un · ub · ud

sun   bun   run   fun

cub   tub   mud   bud

Unit 7 | og · op · ot · ox

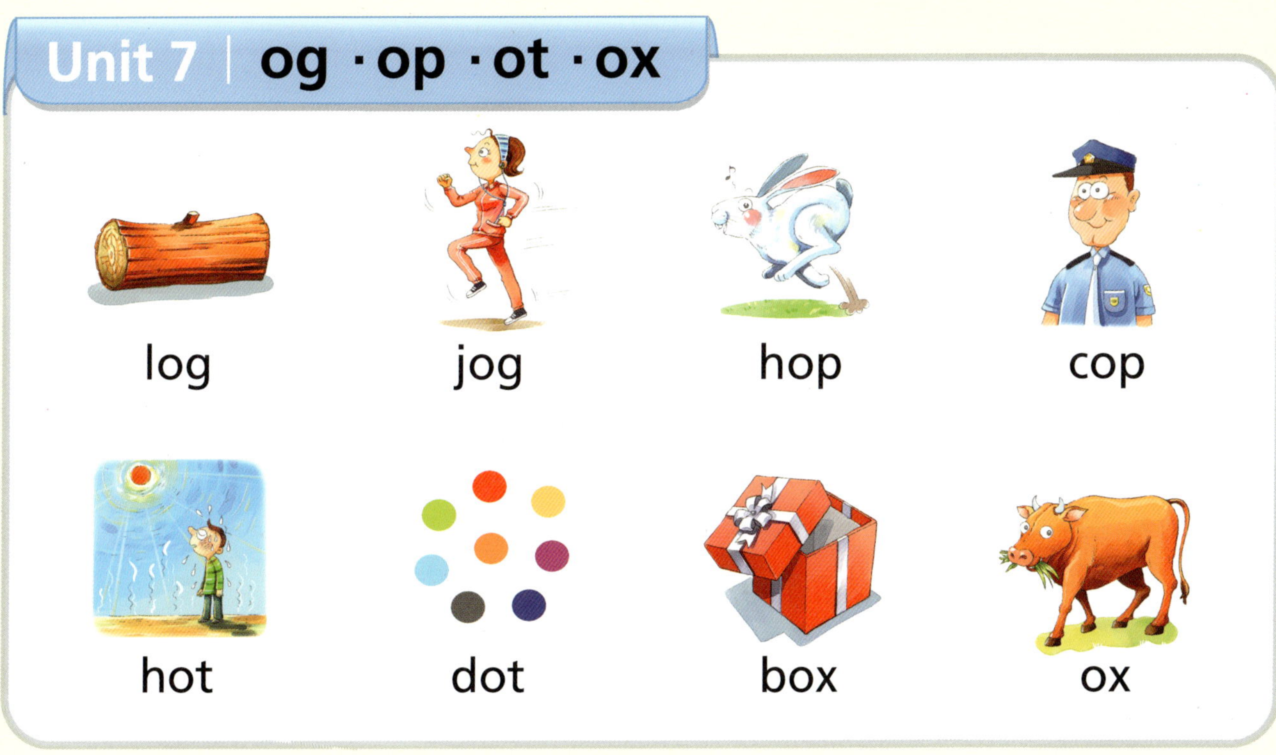

Unit 8 | ed · et · en · elt

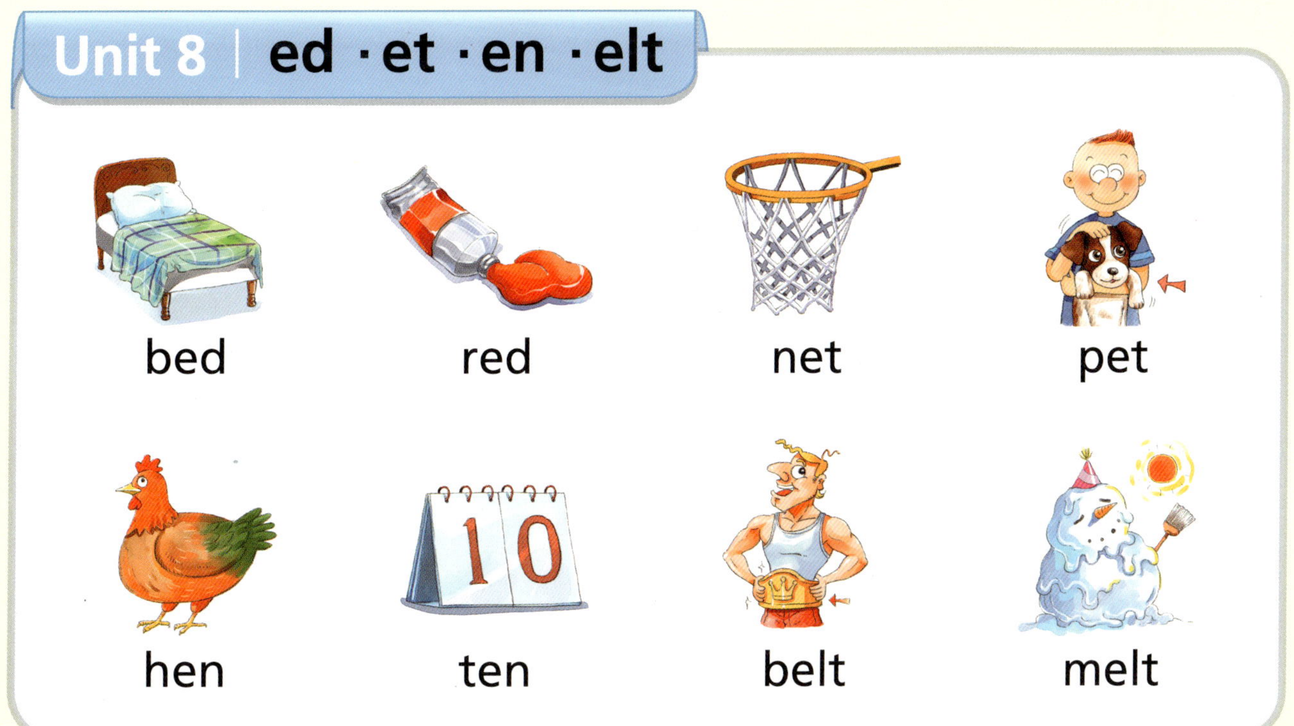

Phonics
wonder

Phonics Wonder

LEVEL 2

Short Vowels

Workbook

YSG Young & Son Global, Inc.

Phonics Wonder

LEVEL 2

Short Vowels

Workbook

Young & Son Global, Inc.

Contents

short vowel a

Look and circle the right ending sound.

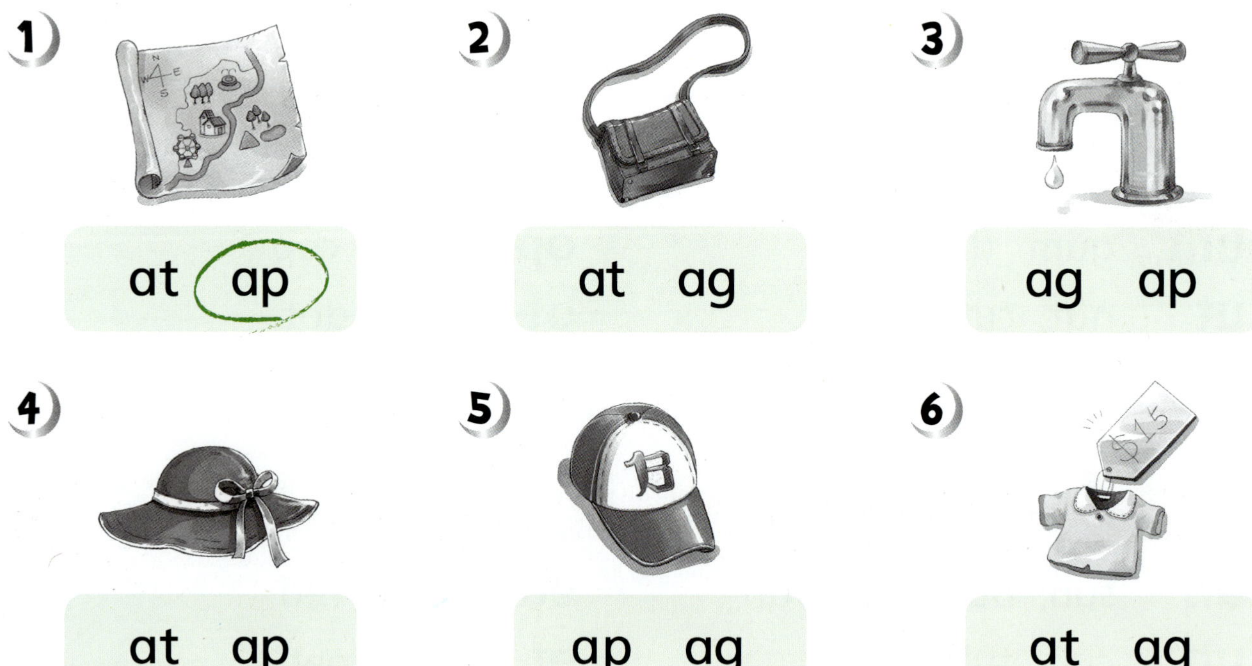

Trace and write the word.

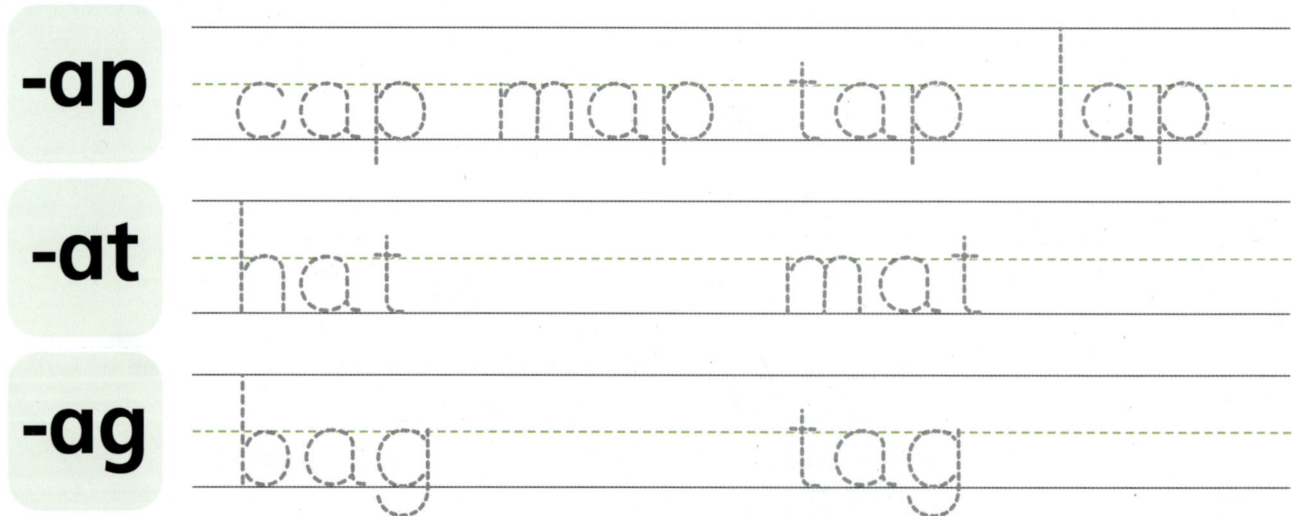

Match and make the word. Then write it.

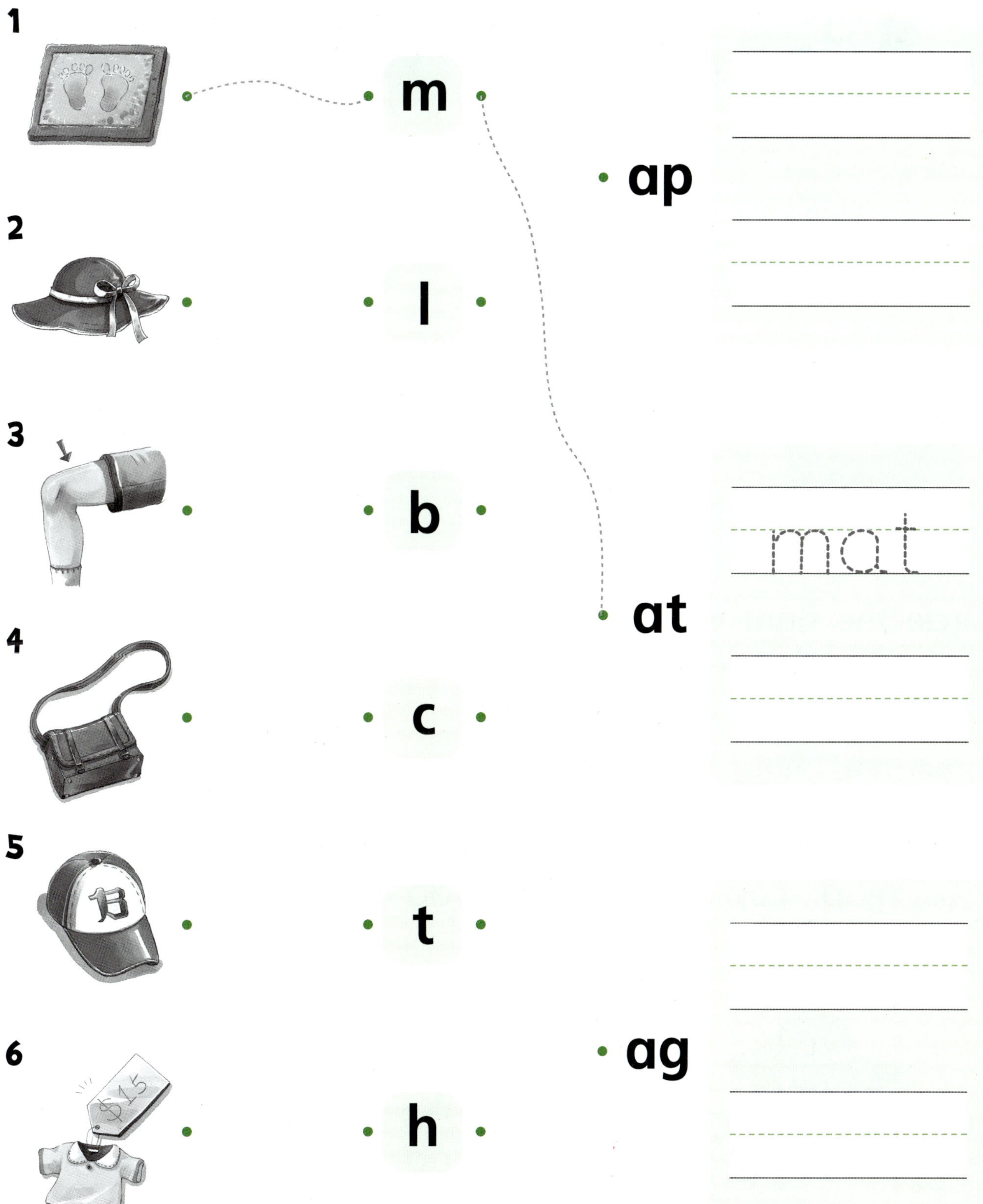

Circle the picture with the same ending sound.

Circle the right word.

Look and write the word.

1 l | ap

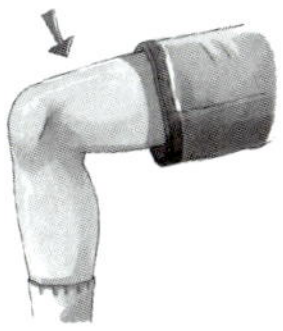

lap   lap

2 t | ap

3 c | ap

4 m | ap

5 h | at

6 m | at

7 b | ag

8 t | ag

short vowel a

Look and circle the right ending sound.

 1)

an   am

2)

am   ad

3)

am   an

4)

ad   am

5)

ad   an

6)

am   an

Trace and write the word.

-an	man can pan fan
-ad	dad sad
-am	ham jam

Match and make the word. Then write it.

1

h

· an

2

m

3

s

· ad

4

p

5

j

· am

6

d

Circle the picture with the same ending sound.

Circle the right word.

Look and write the word.

1  f an

2  c an

3  p an

4  m an

5  d ad

6  s ad

7  h am

8  j am

Look and circle the right word.

1 

can
cap
tag

2 

map
fan
hat

3 

bag
ham
mat

4 

man
sad
jam

Look and circle the right picture.

1 man      

2 dad     

3 ham     

Match and make the word. Then write it.

1 

t • • an

____

2 

f • • ap

____

3 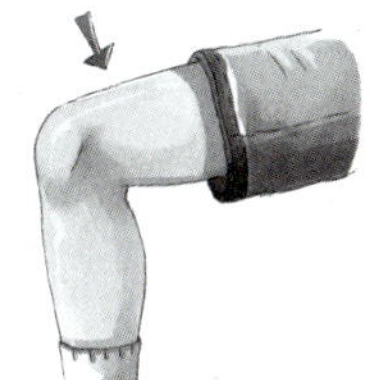

l • • am

____

4 

m • • ag

____

5 

s • • at

____

6 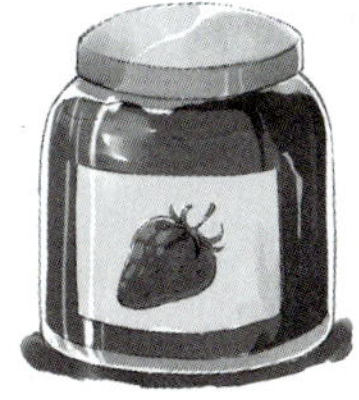

j • • ad

____

Circle the right word and write it.

1) can / cap — *can*

2) tag / tap

3) man / lap

4) mat / sad

5) pan / dad

6) cap / jam

7) hat / ham

8) fan / pan

Circle the picture with the same ending sound.

1  

2  

3  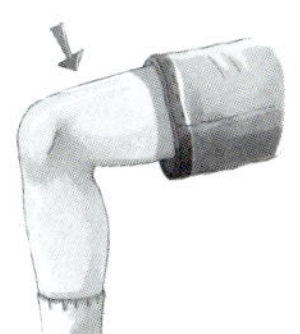

4  

Look and write the word.

1) 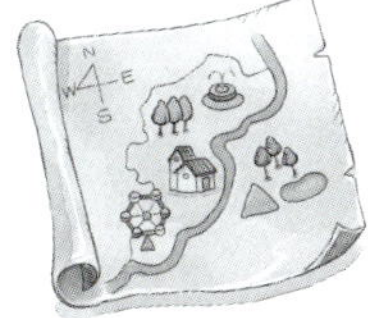 _______________

2)  _______________

3)  _______________

4)  _______________

5)  _______________

6)  _______________

Unit 3 short vowel i

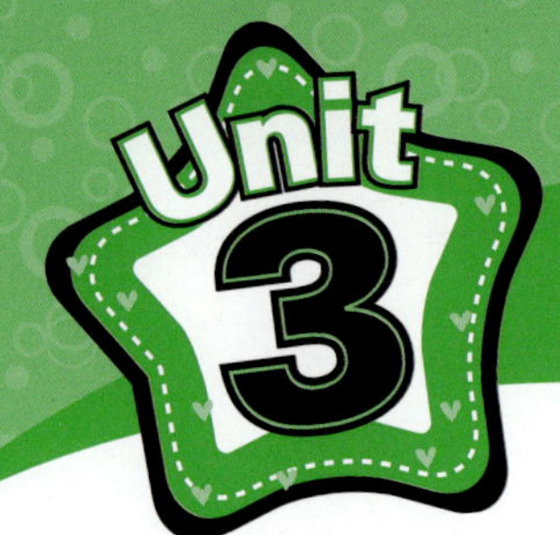

Match the picture to the right ending sound.

1 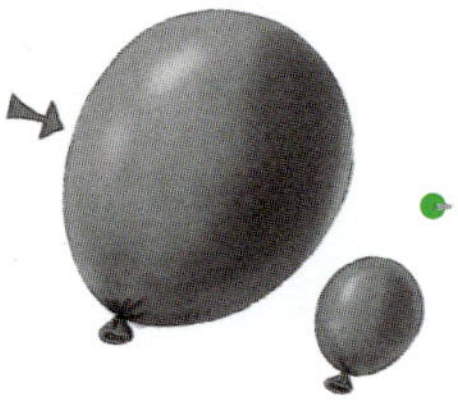

2 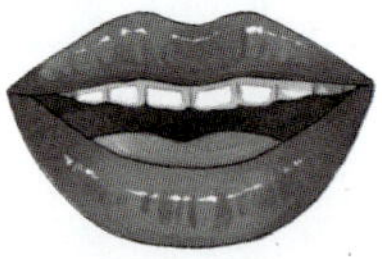

3 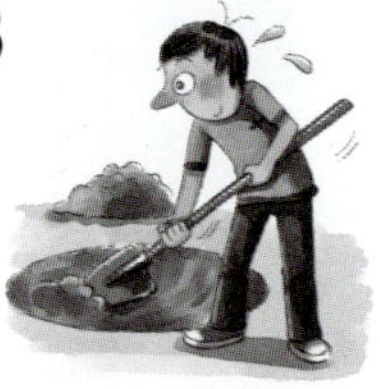

4 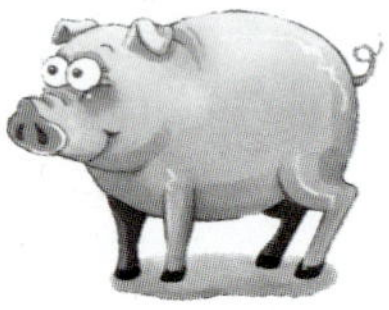

-ig

-ip

5 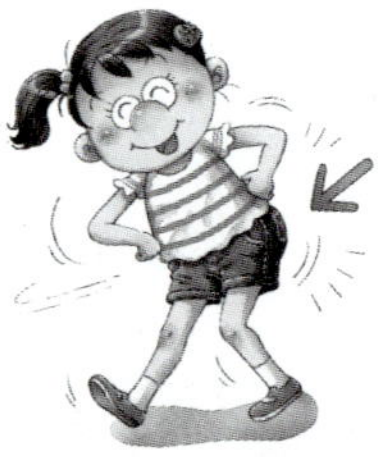

6 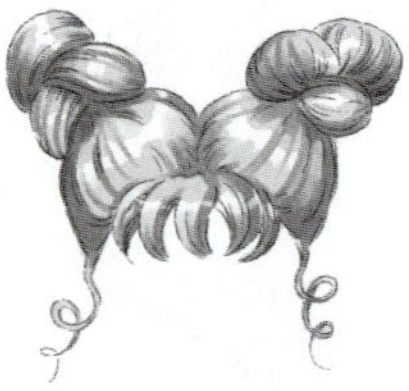

7 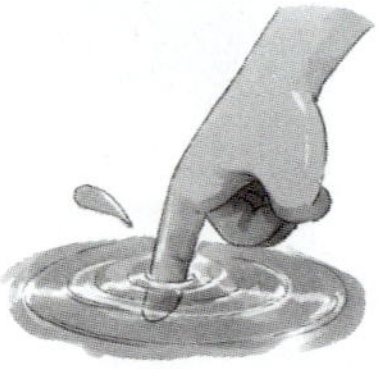

8 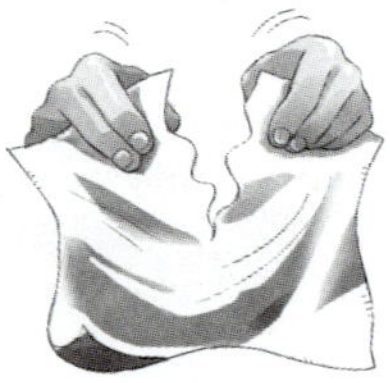

Trace and write.

-ig big pig dig wig

-ip hip lip rip dip

Match and make the word. Then write it.

1

p •

• ig ___________

____

• ip ___________

2

d •

• ig ___________

____

• ip ___________

3

h •

• ig ___________

____

• ip ___________

4

l •

• ig ___________

____

• ip ___________

5

w •

• ig ___________

____

• ip ___________

6

r •

• ig ___________

____

• ip ___________

Check the right picture.

1 wig

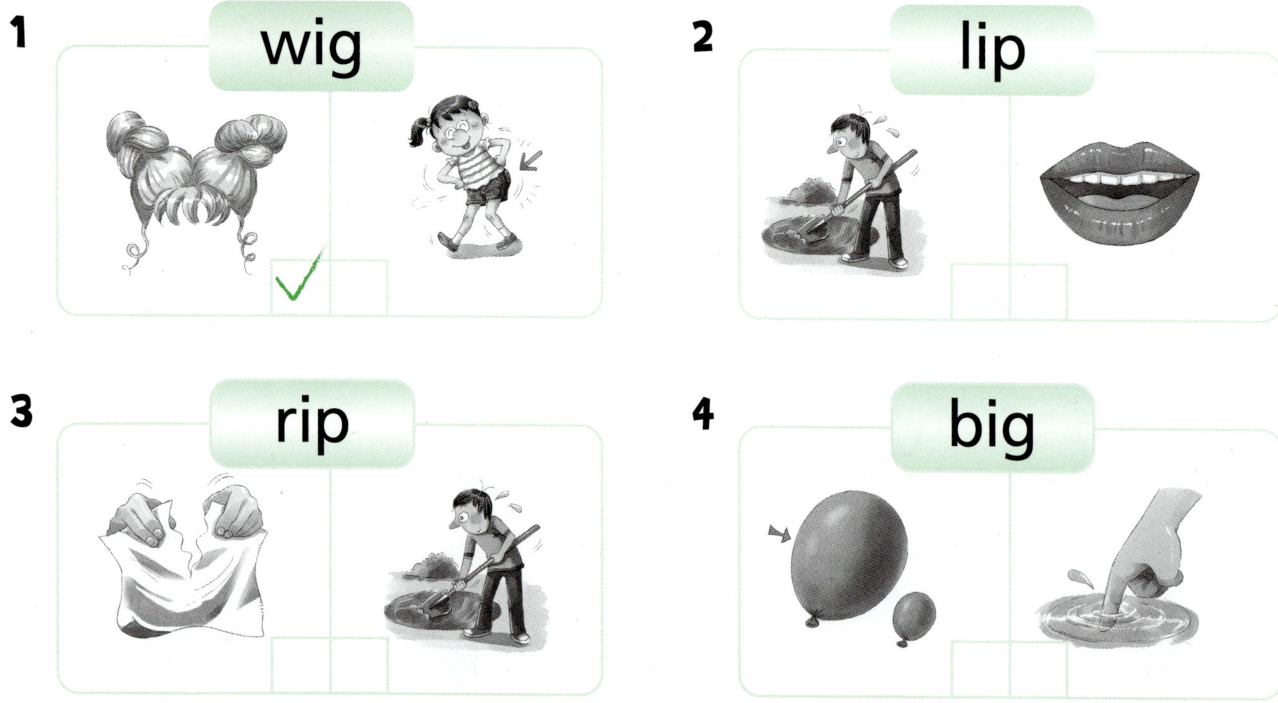

2 lip

3 rip

4 big

Circle the right word.

1) t d i g s p

2) w p g h i p

3) d m l i p t

4) p i g l n g

5) c d i p z g

6) d f n w i g

Look and write the word.

1 b | ig

2 p | ig

3 d | ig

4 w | ig

5 h | ip

6 l | ip

7 d | ip

8 r | ip

short vowel i

Match the picture to the right ending sound.

1 

2 

3 

4 

-in

-id

-it

 5

 6

 7

 8

Trace and write.

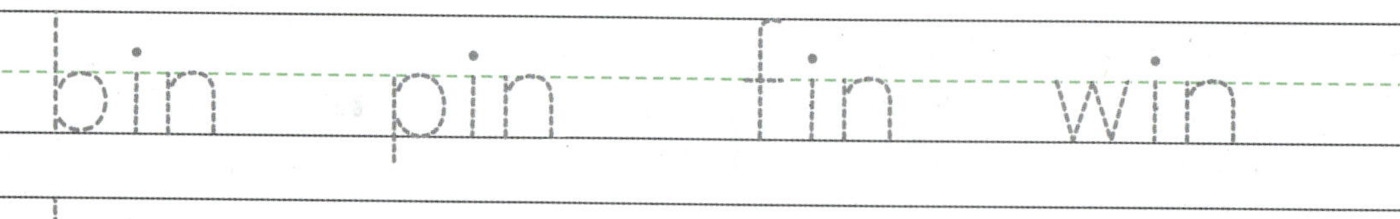

-in   bin   pin   fin   win

-it   hit   sit

-id   lid   kid

Match and make the word. Then write it.

1

b

- in
- it

____

____

2

h

- it
- id

____

____

3

f

- it
- in

____

____

4

l

- id
- it

____

____

5

w

- ig
- in

____

____

6

k

- id
- ip

____

____

Check the right picture.

Circle the right word.

Look and write the word.

1 f | in

2 b | in

3 w | in

4 p | in

5 s | it

6 h | it

7 k | id

8 l | id

Look and circle the right word.

1 

big
dig
dip

2 

fin
hip
rip

3 

bin
win
sit

4 

wig
kid
pin

Look and circle the right picture.

1 

hit

2 

lid

 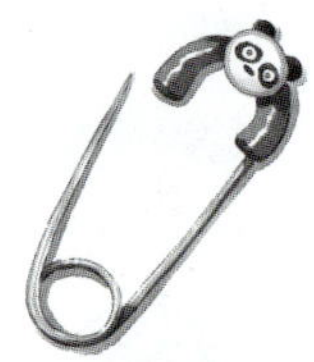 

3

dip

Match and make the word. Then write it.

1 　　l •　　• ig

2 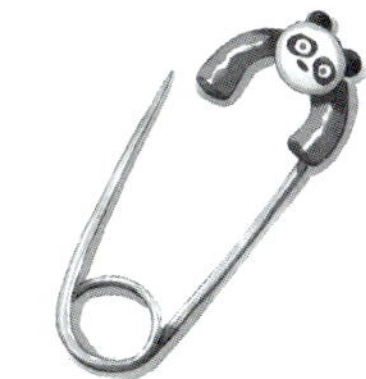　　p •　　• ip

3 　　s •　　• in

4 　　k •　　• it

5 　　p •　　• id

6 　　h •　　• ip

Circle the right word and write it.

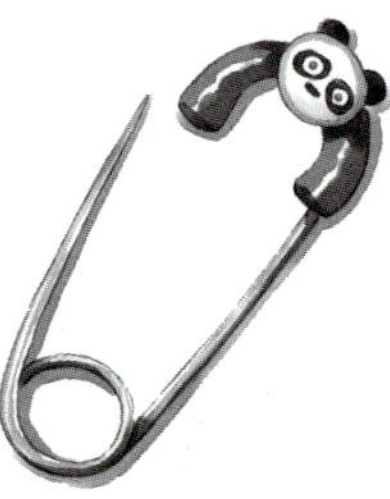

1)

pin
fin

____

2)

hit
sit

____

3)

kid
pig

____

4)

lip
rip

____

5)

dig
win

____

6)

lid
dip

____

7)

big
wig

____

8)

bin
hip

____

Circle the picture with the same ending sound.

Look and write the word.

short vowel U

Look and circle the right ending sound.

 1) 

ug   ut

2) 

um   ug

3)

um   ut

4)

ut   um

5) 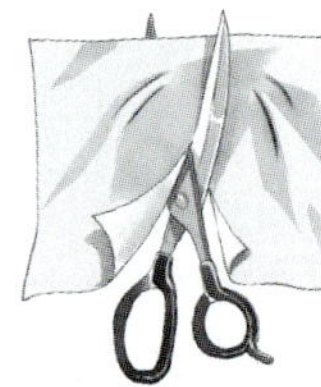

ug   um

6)

ug   ut

Trace and write the word.

-ug	bug rug mug hug
-um	gum drum
-ut	nut cut

Match and make the word. Then write it.

1

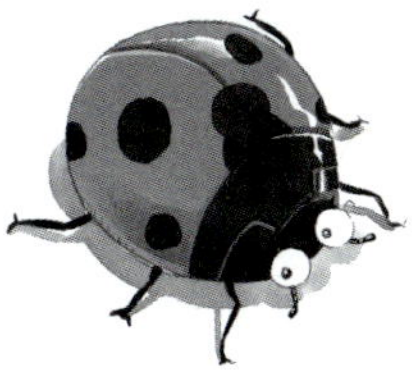

n

ut

2

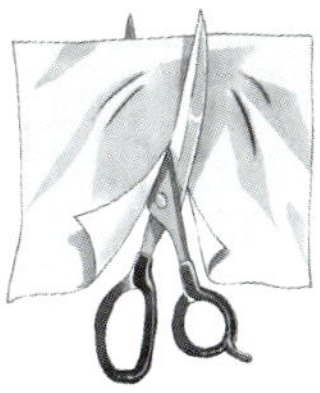

dr

3

c

um

4

b

5

g

ug

6

m

Circle the picture with the same ending sound.

1

2

3

Circle the right word.

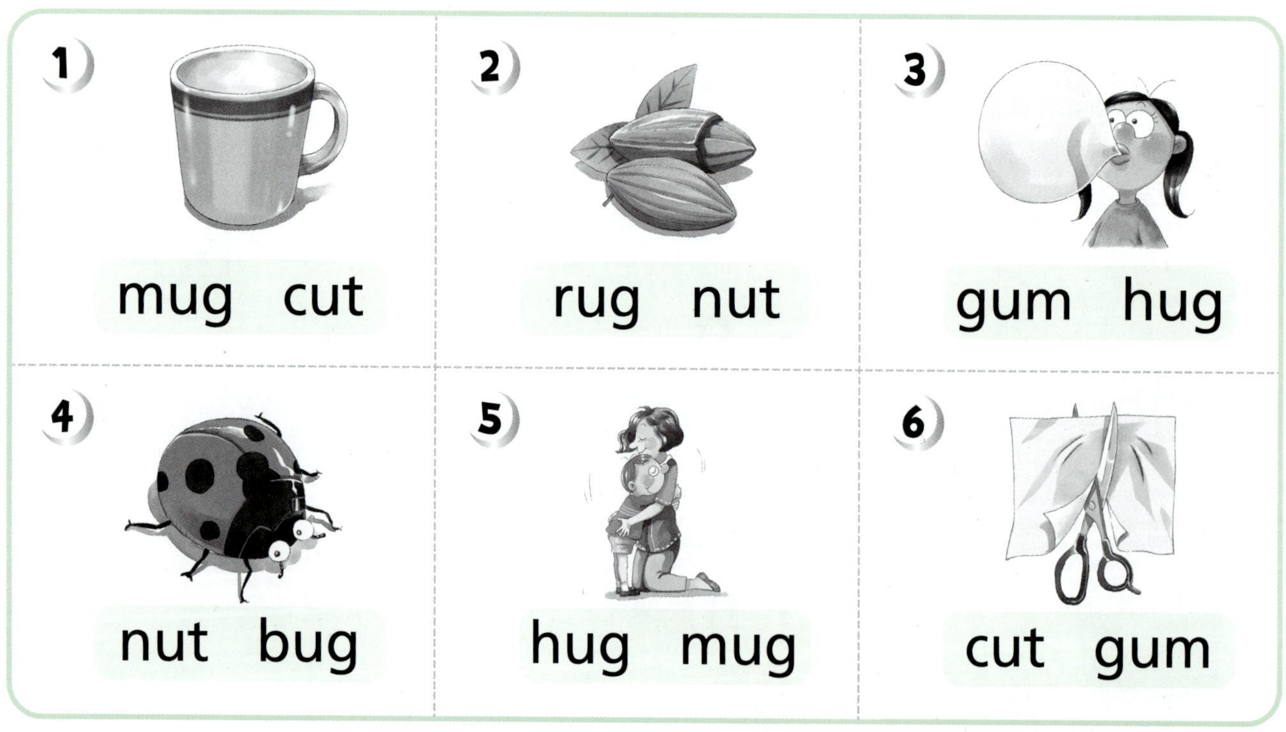

1) mug   cut

2) rug   nut

3) gum   hug

4) nut   bug

5) hug   mug

6) cut   gum

Look and write the word.

1 b | ug

2 m | ug

3 r | ug

4 h | ug

5 g | um

6 dr | um

7 n | ut

8 c | ut

Unit 6 short vowel u

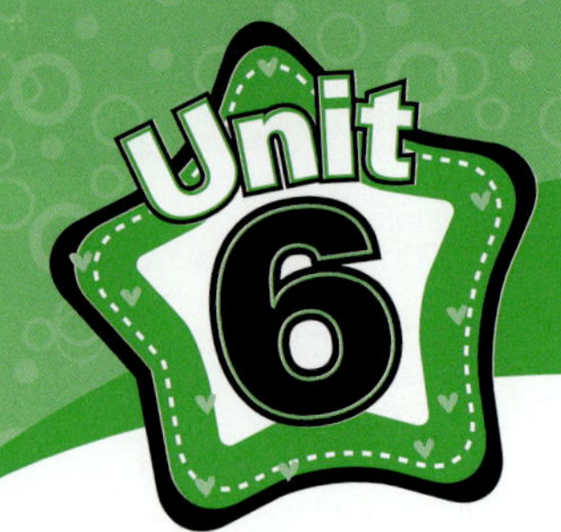

Look and circle the right ending sound.

1)

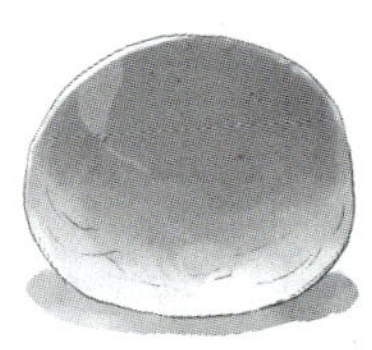

un ub

2)

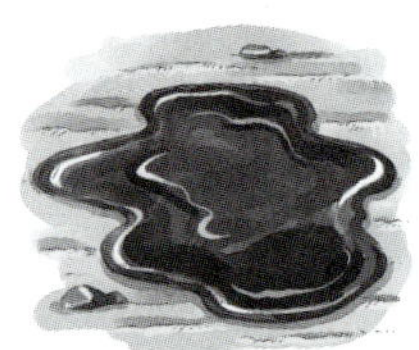

ub ud

3)

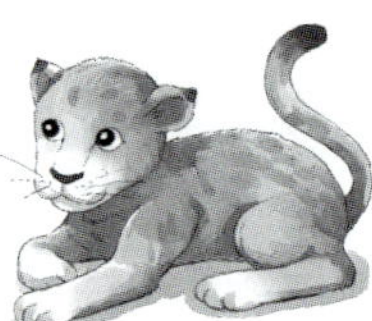

un ub

4)

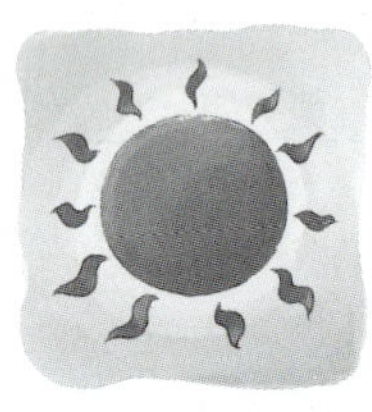

ub un

5)

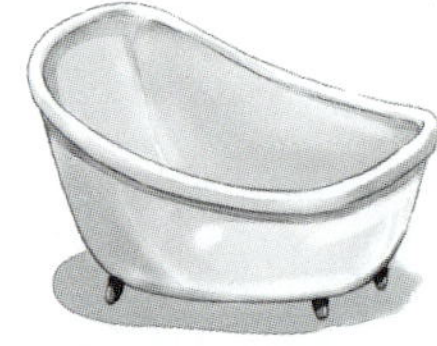

ud ub

6)

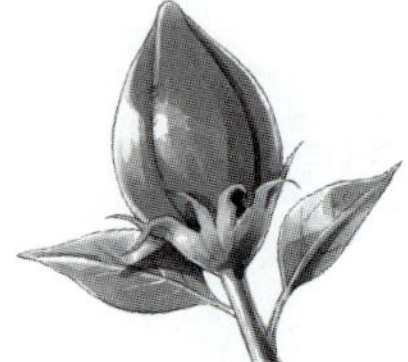

un ud

Trace and write the word.

-un sun bun run fun

-ub cub tub

-ud mud bud

Match and make the word. Then write it.

1

c

un
____

2

s

3

m

ub
____

4

b

5
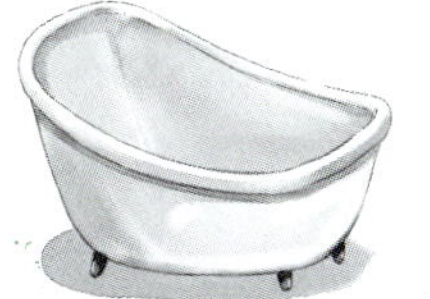
t

ud
____

6

r

Circle the picture with the same ending sound.

1

2

3

Circle the right word.

Look and write the word.

1. s | un

2. f | un

3. b | un

4. r | un

5. c | ub

6. t | ub

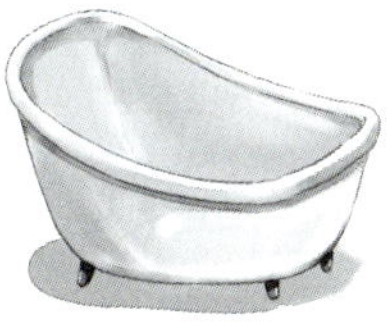

7. m | ud

8. b | ud

Look and circle the right word.

1 
bug
bun
bud

2 
mug
tub
gum

3 
fun
nut
hug

4 
bud
tub
drum

Look and circle the right picture.

1  sun

2  cub
 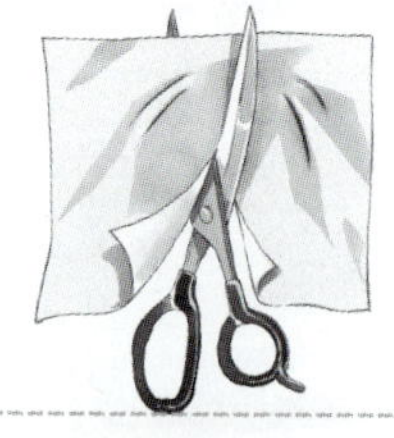 

3 mud

Find and circle the word. Then write it.

s t u b j c b u d e r c f u n t f p o n

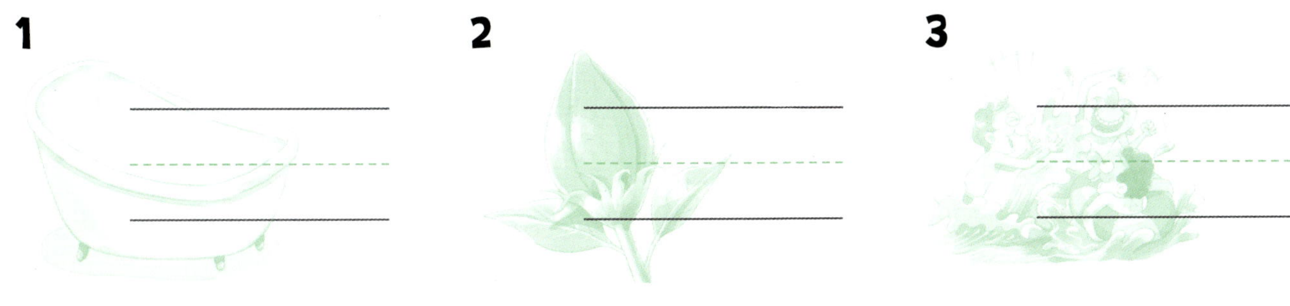

1   **2**   **3**

t i g u m j c u b b a n r c b k a h u g

4   **5**   **6**

m u g r s h e c u t v j n d r u m k l t

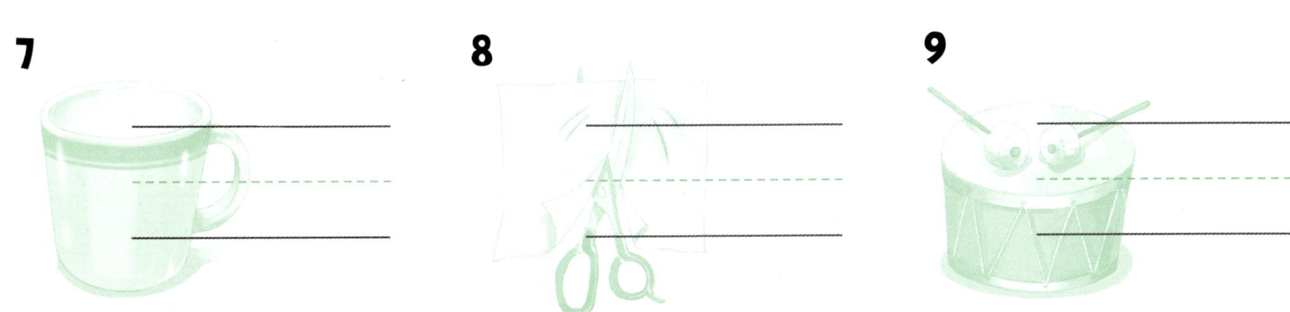

7   **8**   **9**

Look and write the missing letters.

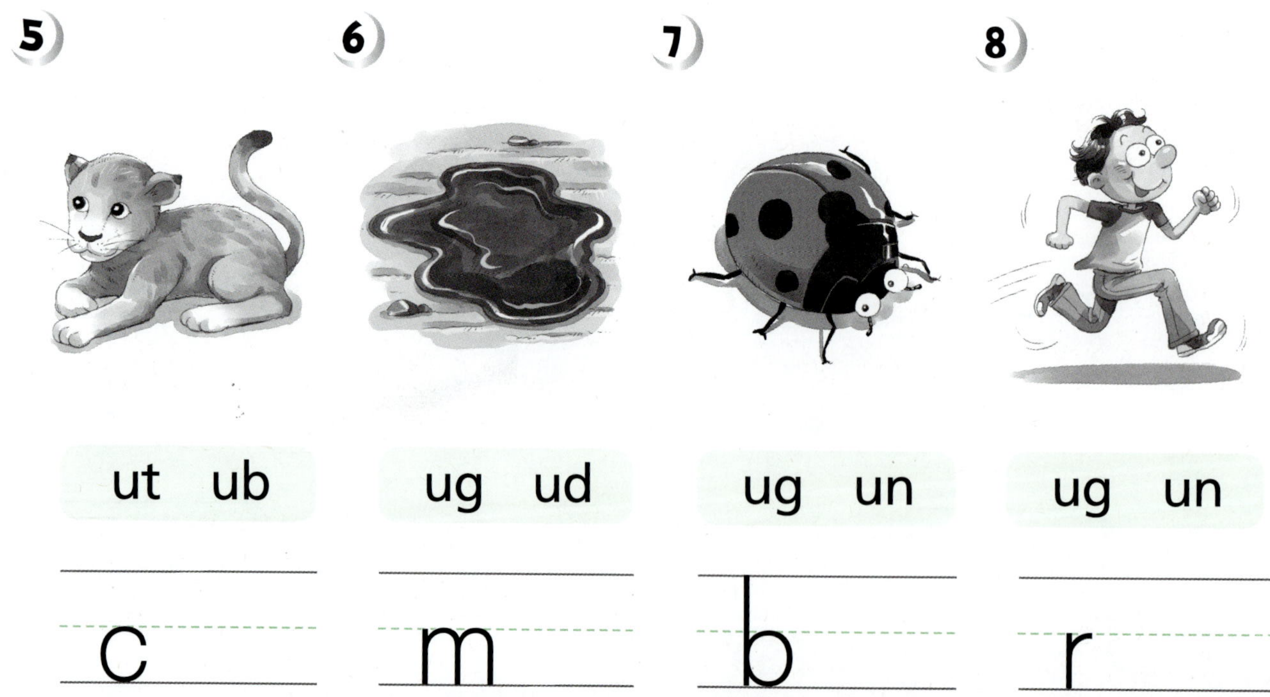

38

Circle the picture with the given ending sound.

1 -un

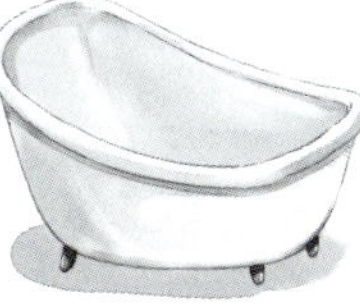

2 -ug

3 -um

4 -ut

Look and write the word.

1) 

2) 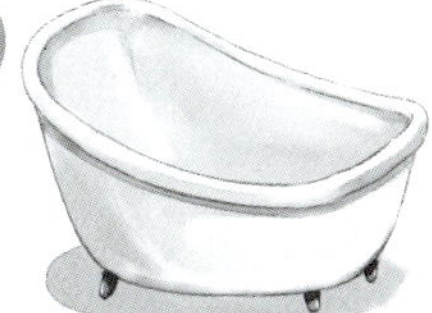

3) 

4) 

5) 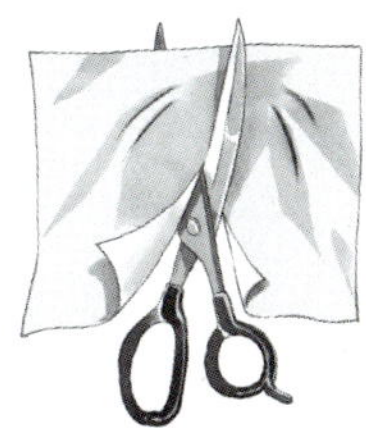

6) 

short vowel o

Unit 7

Match the given ending sound to the pictures.

1) -ox **2)** -og **3)** -op **4)** -ot

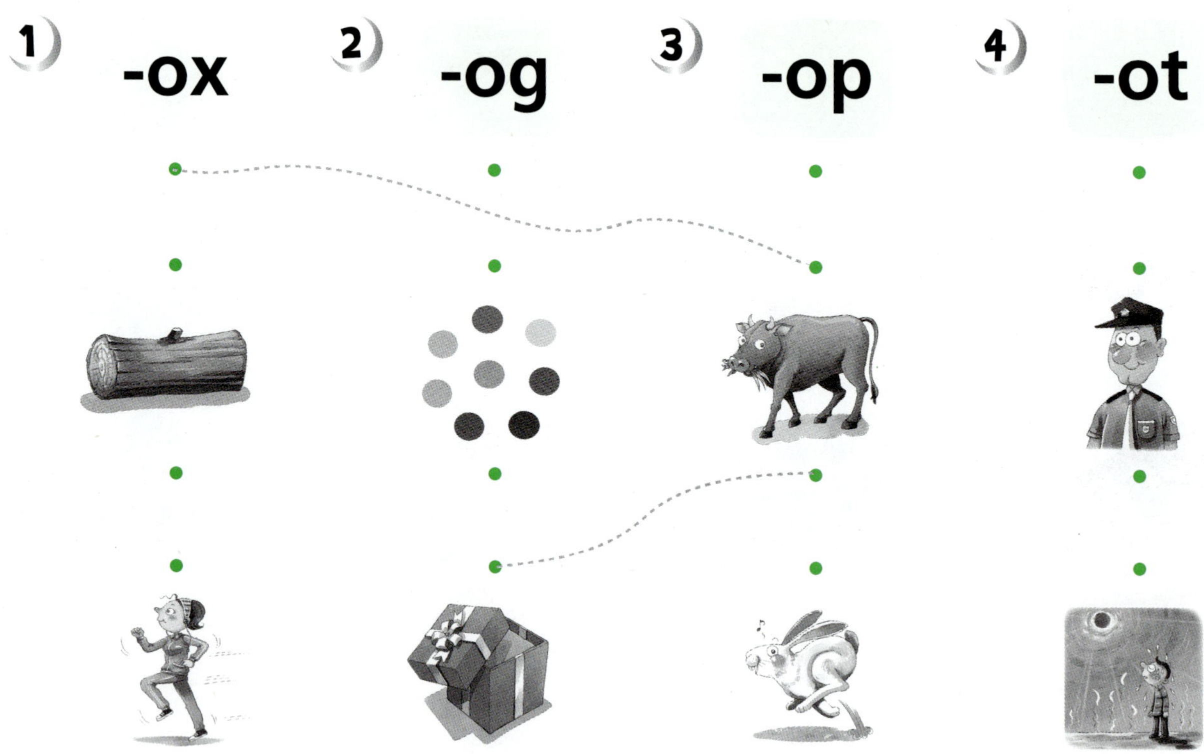

Trace and write.

-og	log	jog
-op	hop	cop
-ot	hot	dot
-ox	box	ox

Match and make a word. Then write it.

1

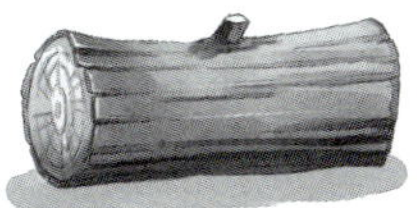

l •

- og
- op
- ot

____

2

h •

- og
- op
- ox

____

3

b •

- op
- ot
- ox

____

4

d •

- og
- ot
- ox

____

5

j •

- og
- ot
- ox

____

6

h •

- og
- op
- ot

____

Check the right picture.

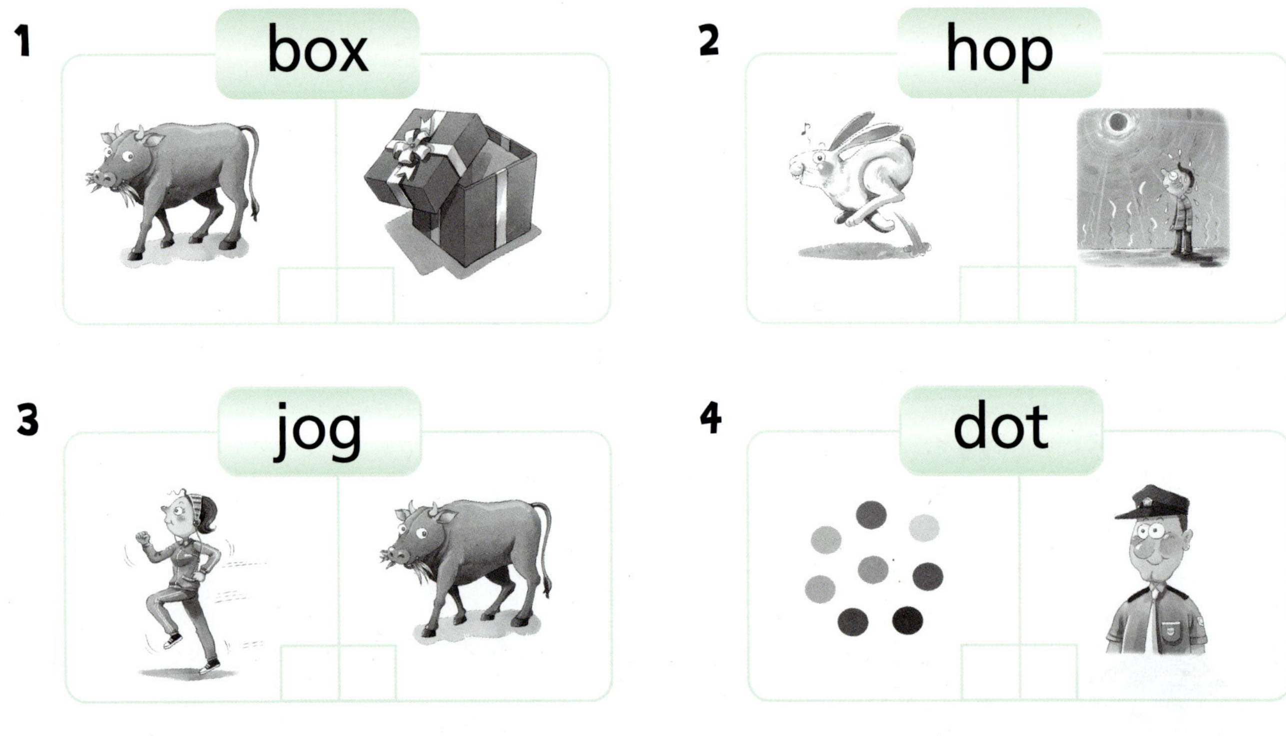

Circle the right word.

Look and write the word.

1   j | og

2   l | og

3 | ox

4   b | ox

5   c | op

6   h | op

7   h | ot

8   d | ot

short vowel e

Match the given ending sound to the pictures.

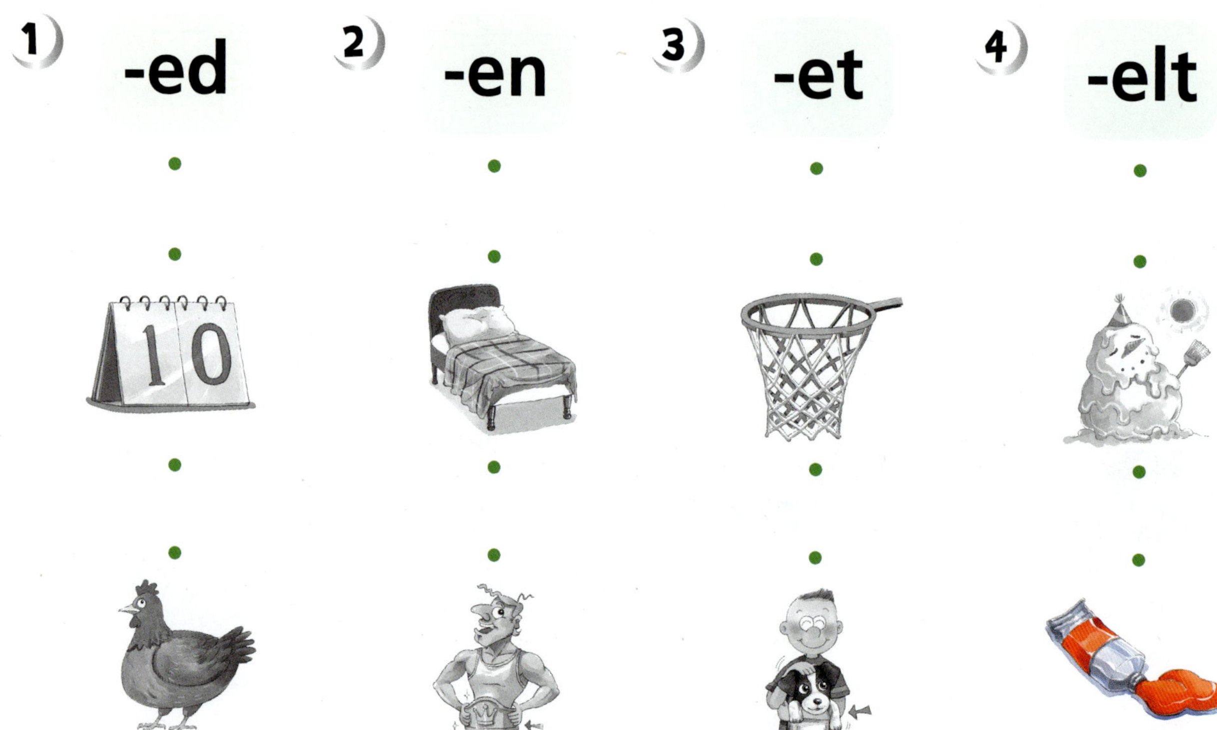

Trace and write.

-ed	bed	red
-et	net	pet
-en	hen	ten
-elt	belt	melt

Match and make a word. Then write it.

1

b •

- ed
- et
- en

2

n •

- ed
- et
- elt

3

p •

- et
- en
- elt

4

h •

- ed
- en
- elt

5

b •

- ed
- et
- elt

6

r •

- ed
- et
- en

Check the right picture.

1 melt

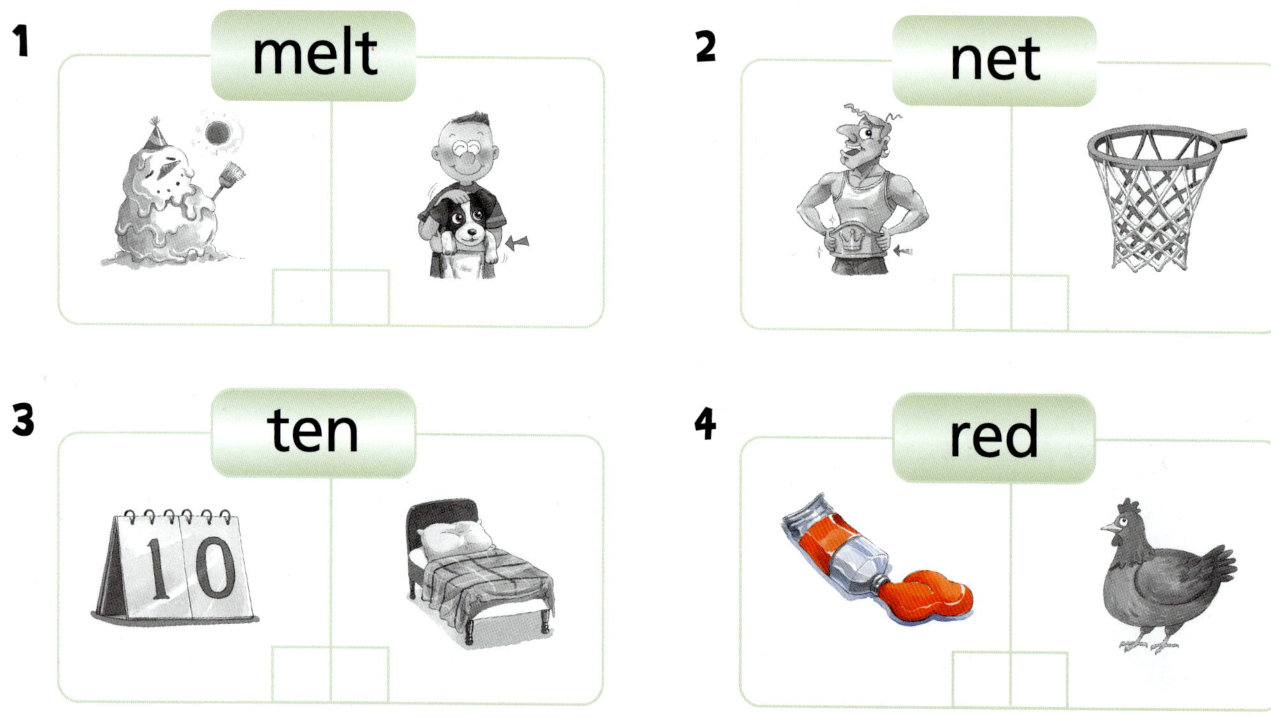

2 net

3 ten

4 red

Circle the right word.

1) psbedg

2) pethjt

3) henrcp

4) fpbelt

5) hredkt

6) meltpb

Look and write the word.

1 b | ed _______________

2 r | ed _______________

3 n | et _______________

4 p | et _______________

5 t | en _______________

6 h | en _______________

7 m | elt _______________

8 b | elt _______________

Look and circle the right word.

 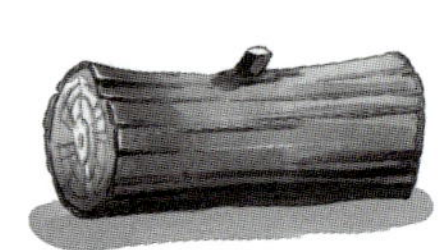

log
jog
hop

box
cop
dot

red
bed
hen

net
belt
melt

Look and circle the right picture.

1 hot 

2 box 

3 hen 
 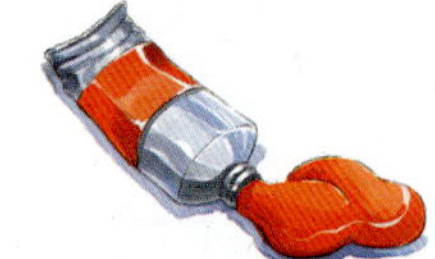

4 belt 

Find and circle the word. Then write it.

j m e l t v u w t e n m a n v o x y h i

1

2

3

d e b e d k h o t i g c u n p e t l m z

4

5

6

y e j o g u j r e d w e f n i h o p h n

7

8

9

Look and write the missing letters.

 1) 

op   en

h

 2) 

et   elt

b

3) 

ot   og

d

4) 

og   et

l

5) 

ed   et

b

6) 

ox   en

b

7)  

et   elt

p

8) 

ox   op

c

Circle the picture with the given ending sound.

1 

2 -ed

3 -en

4 -op

   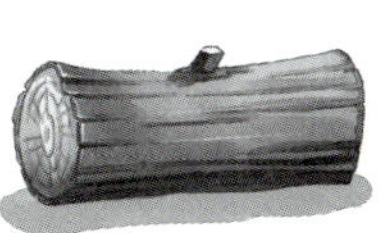

Look and write the word.

1)  _______________________

2)  _______________________

3)  _______________________

4)  _______________________

5)  _______________________

6)  _______________________

Phonics Wonder

LEVEL 2

Short Vowels